AN INNOCENT GROWS UP

AN INNOCENT GROWS UP

Norman Hancock

J. M. DENT AND SONS LTD.

Made in Great Britain

by

The Temple Press · Letchworth · Herts.

First published 1947

LITHOGRAPH BY JOHN PIPER

5.368.

FOREWORD

In this autobiographical study of immaturity, nearly all names and places are disguised, an occasional liberty has been taken with the chronological order of events, and some of the minor characters are composite portraits.

Finally, a personal note. I have included in these pages only those members of my family necessary to the presentation of a self-portrait in childhood and youth. I trust that those who are omitted will accept my assurance that their exclusion was determined by the nature of the book's structure and design, and in no way indicates lack of goodwill or personal regard.

N. H.

CONTENTS

I MAKE AN UNCERTAIN ENTRY

WHEN I look back upon the days of my childhood that period does not seem remote—rather it seems to lie alongside my present existence, a fully developed picture in which everything is of normal size—the houses and streets of the town in which I lived, the people with whom I came in contact, all assume everyday dimensions. Only the figure of myself is dwarfed; like a small but constant shadow it moves, as it were, along a parallel course to the present, keeping pace with my growth and development.

I was born in 1894 at Chiswick, London, and when I was two years old my mother and father moved to the west country to take over a retail drapery business in a small Somerset town. They had staked their all upon the success of this venture. My father, after spending years of drudgery in the employ of others, had at last the opportunity to run a business of his own.

Within a few weeks of our arrival in the new home I presented him with an additional anxiety—I was taken seriously and dangerously ill. A growth in my throat developed so rapidly that the pressure on my windpipe threatened to choke me. A tracheotomy was performed and a silver tube inserted in my throat through which I breathed. The operation, though successful, had a considerable effect upon my health and constitution. Born under weight and delicate from the moment of birth, I was a very sickly-looking creature indeed. A detached onlooker observing my puny body, my small lolling head, and my matchstick limbs, might well have wondered if such a specimen were worthy of preservation. Fate, in fact, came almost to the same conclusion, for shortly after the operation an incident occurred which threatened to put an end to my brief existence. Breathing through a tube in one's neck is not an easy or natural business, and my parents had employed a young nursemaid to attend me. It was this young woman's job to see that my position was such as to make the process as easy as possible. Even in the most comfortable position I made no great success of it, but took the air into my lungs with strain and shuddering convulsions, making a most unpleasant noise as phlegm from my throat bubbled and whistled in the metal tube. After a few hours the tube would become congested with mucus and it was necessary to take it out and clean it. Naturally it had to be done quickly and efficiently, since without the tube I could scarcely breathe at all. On one such occasion the nursemaid was unable to replace the tube and observing that my face had commenced to turn black, she ran from the room shouting for help. My father, hearing her cries, rushed upstairs and managed to force the tube into position just in time to prevent my suffocation.

After this setback I began to make satisfactory progress and eventually, when the scars had healed, the tube was removed, but to this day I still have a hole in my throat, twisted vocal cords, and a defective sound-box which sometimes gives out at the most embarrassing moments.

CHAPTER II

CORNHILL HOUSE

OUR house faced the market square and was known as Cornhill House. Drapery houses in the provinces adopted such names, hoping perhaps by the implied association to increase their commercial status. Other such titles included London House, Manchester House, Bon Marché, and the like.

Cornhill House was a large rambling place; in addition to the shop, which occupied most of the ground floor, it had fourteen rooms, a kitchen and scullery, and a great cavernous recess where the coal was kept—not to mention huge cupboards which in themselves were almost the size of rooms. One especially was so large that three people might have occupied it with comfort except that having no window it was dark and airless. Sometimes if I was unruly or misbehaved myself my parents would threaten to imprison me in the 'windowless room,' and though I knew the threat to be an idle one, the very thought of being shut in that forbidding chamber was sufficient to achieve my correction.

At the back of the house the ground rose steeply—so steeply that the sprawling garden seemed to hang over us—and when I stood looking out of the french window of the dining-room I could see trees and bushes tilted forward as if they were charging down upon me. Because of the sloping ground the kitchen window looked out on a level with the street. Wagons descending this street were put on the 'drag'; a metal block or 'chuck,' attached to the bottom of the wagon

by a chain, was slipped under a wheel to act as a brake
and to relieve the pressure on the horses.   I liked to
climb on a chair beneath the window to see the sparks
fly as the metal dragged over the flinty road.   It left
a shining track on the roadway, as though a giant
snail had just crawled by.

To me the most interesting part of the house was
the top floor.   It was reached by a winding staircase,
narrow and uneven.   At a turn in the stairs was a
door which opened upon a lumber-room.   In here
was an accumulation of rejected fittings from the
shop—brass rods, boxes, show-stands, glass shelves,
and most important of all, for they were morbidly
fascinating, tailors' dummies shaped approximately to
the female form with narrow waists and protuberant
bosoms.   Some had once been complete with waxen
heads, but the heads had become detached and now
stood in a row on a shelf smiling inanely at their
truncated bodies.   I seldom looked into the room
for long.   It was a Bluebeard's chamber, silent and
secret; even the daylight advanced with diffidence
through the grimy single-paned window.

On the top floor were the bedrooms of the assistants
to which entrance was gained by two long landings
running the entire length of the house and connected
in the middle by a bridge.   On the one side was the
room of Mr. Tomkins of the gents' outfitting department; on the other the sleeping quarters of the 'young
ladies.'   Mr. Tomkins was constrained by a gentleman's agreement to keep to his own side of the
building.   Thus the connecting bridge became a
'bridge of sighs' joining but never (so far as was
known) uniting the opposite sexes.

Actually the bridge was forbidden to me also—my
mother thought it dangerous—but the excitement of
looking downstairs into the deepest recesses of the

house and seeing the main staircase tilted at an unfamiliar angle was an irresistible attraction.

In the summer I spent long hours in the garden. There was a lawn partly surrounded by trees and laurel bushes. Jim, our errand boy, showed me how to put the leaves of these bushes on the mouth against the tongue and, pursing the lips, produce a loud, penetrating whistle.

Beyond the lawn the garden rose steeply for a considerable distance. For some reason my father had planted a very large number of currant bushes—there must have been dozens of them. When the fruit was in season I enjoyed wandering in and out of these bushes and sampling the produce. I liked the strong, musky odour of the black currants, but it was the white that I ate—the red taking second place. There were also apple-trees and one very large William pear which my mind associated with the travelling fair because the fair came to the town shortly after the pears had been gathered from the tree.

On one side of the garden was a shirt factory in which hundreds of girls worked at sewing-machines. The noise of these machines filled the air with a perpetual buzz, and as I sat idle or drowsing in the sunshine it seemed as though a swarm of bees kept me company. On very hot days the doors of the factory were open and I was able to see the girls stitching the shirts, their feet rising and falling in constant motion upon the pedals of the machines. They appeared to be victims of a treadmill, but in actual fact all the machines were driven by an engine, the connecting belt of which I could see high up in the roof lolloping along like a long strip of revolving liquorice.

On the opposite side of the garden a lane ran between stone walls to the top of the hill. On certain mornings a man on a horse came down the lane. Only his head was visible above the garden wall; it bobbed up and down like a piece of rock bouncing slowly down an incline.

This lane was our nearest walk. It turned right at the top of the hill and changed from a stony track to a mossy path which led between thick overhanging trees. Ferns of every description lined its banks and strange flowers, fungi, and poisonous plants rioted in the damp earth. Even in the heat of summer the path was damp and spongy and rotting leaves gave to the atmosphere the not unpleasant odour of decay.

I remember best the seasons of sunshine and warmth; perhaps the mind slurs over the memory of winter when, confined to a room, I whiled the hours away with my paint-box and building bricks. I had a nursery and my father had built me a rocking-horse and a swing. The rocking-horse consisted of two elliptical pieces of wood carved to thin rakish points and joined together by a seat in the middle. Rocked at high speed, the whole contrivance would move across the floor by the force of momentum and thus provide an added excitement. The swing was suspended in the open doorway and if daringly manipulated would carry me out over the well of the stairs.

With winter came colds, coughs, and sore throats, and to fatten me up and to 'keep up my strength' I was put on a course of cod-liver oil. Also every morning at eleven o'clock I had an additional meal which consisted of a plate of hot bacon fat mopped up with bread. For a sore throat my mother would wrap an old stocking turned inside out round my neck before I went to bed. I liked best the treatment for a cold on the chest. A piece of brown paper warmed before the fire was rubbed with a

Russian tallow candle and then applied to the chest; the warmth was soothing and I enjoyed the strange smell unlike any other that I knew, penetrating and aromatic.

Winter brought the long nights which I did not like because of going up to bed in the semi-darkness. I had to negotiate two flights of stairs and a long passage lit only by a naked gas-jet from which a pale half-moon of yellow flame issued with a thin scream of sound as if whistling to keep up its spirits. To my nervous ear this sound seemed to wax and wane—one moment sighing softly, the next shrieking hysterically as though close behind me.

Hung on the pillars of the landing above the stairs were two black statuettes of negroes with curved swords in their hands. As I mounted the staircase I kept my eyes fixed on these figures in the belief that only by so doing could I prevent them from making a movement.

At the bend in the stairs they were out of sight and I was safe from the orbit of their malevolence. But here a new danger awaited. Behind and slightly to the left of the trilling gas-jet (now at the top note of its shrill warning) was a deep pit of darkness which by day was an innocent but ill-lighted store-room where the reserved shop paper was kept. It was a curious chamber like the shaft of a lift and with a ladder leading down into the crepuscular gloom of its interior. At night it became for me a bottomless pit from which evil ever threatened.

Once past this spot my troubles were over. But at the turn of the stairs and in its close proximity my feet were as lead and I needed all my strength for the final burst of energy that would send me racing across the landing to the security of my room.

Even in my room I was not entirely free from the

fantastic intrusions of the night. Chairs creaked, shadows danced, and though sleep rescued me for a while I would presently enter the land of nightmare—that concentration camp of the mind which cunningly supplies the ingredients of its own terror.

Memories of small incidents and isolated moments in the life at Cornhill House come to me in patches seen through the clouds of later experience. I remember quiet Sunday afternoons in summer when I sat in the cool dining-room and watched the sunlight filter through the high bushes of laurel which grew outside the french window, filling the room with a gentle subdued light. An arrow of sunlight would sometimes pierce a gap in the bushes and strike the ornamental glasses on the mantelpiece so that each prismatic bar of suspended glass reflected the colours of the rainbow.

On the dim wall opposite hung an oil painting depicting the launching of a lifeboat in stormy seas. In the distance, almost engulfed by mountainous waves, could be seen a ship in distress. This conventional picture of remote and, to me, unimaginable tragedy conveyed no impression of horror. On the contrary, by association it had become almost meaningless—a part of my uneventful, day-to-day existence.

I remember too the half-hour on Sunday mornings when I waited for dinner after our return from church. Perhaps because I was wearing my best clothes, or it may be to avoid the bustle in the dining-room, I would go upstairs and sit in the drawing-room, which extended across the front of the house, and from the windows of which beneath tightly bunched Venetian blinds I would gaze out into the market square and watch a few solitary people returning home.

Then tiring of this I would get up and inspect the

photographs of relations which—mounted in a variety of frames ranging from silver to stained oak, according to their respective importance in the family hierarchy —stood in neat yet informal array upon brackets, mantelpiece, and occasional tables. The expressions and postures of these photographic figures were fixed and stilted as though confinement in the cold and little-used room had robbed them of vitality.

When finally the dinner bell rang—it was a large hand-bell like a station bell and stood on a special bracket in the hall—the vigorous sound seemed to inject the room with temporary life, but as I closed the door I could almost feel the silence settling down behind me like dust that has been momentarily disturbed.

CHAPTER III

SCHOOL AND PLAY

BECAUSE of my ill health I did not go to school until I was six years old.

After my solitary and confined existence I found it an unusual experience. Although there were only about twenty boys attending the school their numbers as I sat among them seemed a veritable multitude. The junior boys sat in the front row so that they might be under the master's eye, for the head master was the only master and he was obliged to teach two or three groups at the same time. We juniors, about five of us all told, were set to learn the multiplication tables; the seniors in the rows behind were doing history; while those in the last row against the wall were specialists learning shorthand.

While I was chanting softly to myself that six times something was something else (nearly always the wrong something when I was not looking at the book) I was disturbed, or rather counter-attracted, since it was more interesting to listen to what was going on behind me than attend to my own lessons, by the master's voice giving dictation to the shorthand students. I would hear his voice droning some such utterance as this:

'Dear Sir, comma, with reference to yours to hand, semicolon.' His elaborate pronunciation of the various punctuation marks was so fascinating that I sat entranced. In my ignorance, since I had not yet learned to read, I imagined that the strange words were capable of the most romantic meanings. I was particularly impressed by the word 'semicolon,' which had a sonorous sound and occurred so much less frequently than the word 'comma,' which to me as the master rapped it out had a sharp questioning note.

But soon the shorthand dictation was over and the master, after a few words to the historians, would return to the front of the class. I was then obliged to pull myself together and join in the chanting of the multiplication tables. This I enjoyed when done in unison, but feared when a solo performance was expected of me in particular.

To some extent I did eventually master those tables, but my greatest difficulty was in learning to read. At the time I believed I should never accomplish it and that I should be obliged to go through life as a sort of half-wit. I certainly never imagined that I should ever enjoy reading. On the contrary, I thought that of all tasks the most Herculean would be to read a book right through from cover to cover.

I did not enjoy school, neither did I actually dislike it—my nature was too passive to allow of any violent reaction. My nervous apprehension when the master asked me a question made me a figure of fun to my companions, but my schoolmaster had unusual patience and understanding.

'Give him time,' he used to say, as I stood confused and stammering before the class, and conscious of his sympathy I gained composure, and facts which had seemed unconnected clicked into place in my mind and assumed reason and meaning.

Slowly plodding away I finally learnt to read, and this achievement, in addition to creating an immediate interest in weekly 'comics' and adventure yarns, gave me also a measure of confidence in myself. Reading school stories I discovered that there was always a dull boy in the class, and this was helpful and encouraging. It seemed to give me a fixed place in the scheme of things; I was not after all something strange or abnormal.

Thus I learnt early that reading does not always refresh the vision, but sometimes pin-points the emotions and reduces feelings to a standard. A rose may smell as sweet and look as beautiful with a name as without one, but once label it and we know what to expect; its colour, scent, and blossom are no longer a matter of conjecture; the rose has been pinned down to the catalogue.

In spite of growing confidence, I did not acquire knowledge easily and found the effort to memorize pure drudgery. Every week-end we were given the collect for Sunday to learn by heart. My father, hearing me mumbling over the prayer book on Sunday evenings, did his best to assist me by explaining the meanings of the sentences. But words and meanings had a curious knack of separating themselves and pursuing devious routes; or the meaning would, as it were, hover above and just out of reach of the words like a picture out of focus or seen through a distorting lens.

When, for instance, I read the collect for the 25th Sunday after Trinity, 'Stir up, we beseech thee, O Lord, the wills of Thy faithful people; that they, plenteously bringing forth the fruit,' etc., the words 'stir' and 'fruit' were for me the operative words; and I thought of my mother making the Christmas pudding and inviting us all to take a stir. I knew, of course, that the collect had nothing to do with Christmas puddings. Yet I was powerless to prevent the unbidden and unbridled activity of my imagination; and the picture in my mind of my mother and father and myself standing round the kitchen table stirring the pudding was superimposed upon the correct meaning explained to me by my father. The result was not unlike that produced when two photographs are taken on the same film, confusing and grotesque.

The school was situated on the outskirts of the town about half a mile from Cornhill House, and was approached by a street which ran uphill for the greater part of the way. At the top of the hill were the church and churchyard partially hidden by a cluster of elm-trees, in the topmost branches of which rooks built their nests. As autumn approached and the leaves fell the large bulbous-looking nests could be seen attached to the branches of the trees like cankerous growths. The birds themselves, with their hoarse, melancholy cry and funereal appearance, completed the sombre atmosphere of the cemetery where, like almonds on a tipsy-cake, the weather-worn grave-stones staggered at every angle.

Even by day beneath the brightest sunshine, the churchyard was gloomy and uninviting; as evening fell it became sinister. On one occasion I had to traverse it shortly after sunset. I was returning home from the house of a friend where I had been to tea. Twilight blunted the outlines of the church, the motionless trees were dark and brooding, a rising mist distorted the appearance of the gravestones which seemed to float in the vapour, pale and incorporeal. Everything was blanketed in a silence which the sound of my footsteps seemed only to intensify. When in later years I read Pope's words:

> But o'er the twilight groves . . .
> and intermingled graves
> Black melancholy sits, and round her throws
> A death-like silence and a dread repose,

I thought of the churchyard, my stumbling feet, and beating heart.

The walk to and from school presented many diversions. The changing seasons gave to the street new aspects and interests. In the sudden spring showers the houses flicked and danced behind the raindrops like a scene depicted by an early cinematograph. When the rain stopped and the sun shone the buildings regained solidity, the white stone slabs of the pavement steamed in the warmth and quickly dried to a dazzling purity, sometimes patterned here and there by drops of moisture when overhanging green trees, caught by a questing breeze, shook themselves dry like birds that shake their feathers after a bath.

The vagaries of the weather formed a subconscious background to my mind, pleasurable and entrancing. My more conscious activities were devoted to methods of passing the time and shortening the journey. The long inclined street with its stone gutters was admirably suited to games of marbles. I was the proud possessor of a large glass ally marble which contained within its crystal depths fascinating convolutions of coloured threads. What joy to see this prince of marbles running, leaping, and flashing in the sun in combat with the lesser breeds of painted clay!

Sometimes in the long summer evenings, when time was of no consequence, we played on the smooth asphalt of the church lane and as a marble was about to be hit the owner would shout:

'There 's a ring all round 'im.'

This was an unconscious reference to the old superstition that the magic ring of witchcraft protected from harm all that it encompassed.

In the winter, on clear frosty days, I bowled my

hoop. As a learner I started with a wooden hoop, but quickly changed over to one of iron, which in addition to providing more solid sport and greater sound effects, had also the attraction that it could be free-wheeled. The end of the metal hoop stick was curved into a crook which when properly adjusted to the rim of the hoop allowed a free and uninterrupted run.

It was during the summer holidays after my first term at school that I first saw the sea. My parents took me with them on a half-day excursion to Seaton. The trip was arranged on an early-closing day so that my father could accompany us.

He wore his double-breasted navy serge suit and his unorthodox soft felt hat. In those days men wore a bowler on most occasions and in the summer a straw hat or 'boater' was permissible. But the soft trilby was seen rarely except in magazine illustrations of anarchists and other revolutionaries.

My mother wore a light skirt and shirt-blouse and a straw hat tilted slightly over the face; while I was dressed in my best sailor suit and black cotton stockings turned over elastic garters at the knee. These black stockings and my clumsy boots accentuated the thinness of my legs, and a broad-brimmed hat encircled by a ribbon bearing the inscription 'H.M.S. VICTORY' dwarfed my small, pointed features to elfin dimensions.

The train jogged cheerfully along the wide valley of the Axe in the bright sunshine. Though the carriage windows were open there was little air moving and the clanking of the engine couplings beat a constant tattoo upon the silence of the countryside. Light streamed down from the sky, and trees, hedges, and cattle stood out with a stereoscopic clarity. The sunshine was so strong upon the fields that they seemed to be drenched in liquid golden paint.

As we approached Seaton I saw the sea intensely blue, flat, and still, as though a section of the sky had been pegged down between the hills which bounded the valley.

When we emerged from the railway station my eyes were dazzled by the white plastered walls of the houses on the sea-front which, unlike our brown sandstone houses at home, met the luminous air as an equal and gave light for light.

We climbed the steep beach, slipping and scuffling among the large loose pebbles, and then when we reached the top of the ridge I saw in all its immensity the great expanse of water stretching from headland to headland and beyond to the horizon. Somnolent, and almost motionless beneath the enervating heat of the sun, it suggested a sense of power that was almost frightening. I stood gazing at it, my senses overwhelmed by its volume and size; and then presently I looked down to where a few yards away at the water's edge small waves moved upon the shingle so softly that the sound of their gentle impact was almost imperceptible—a tiny echo of sound that fell upon the ear like an involuntary sigh.

The contrast was striking, it was as though a giant was practising a playful caress; and now I was no longer frightened by it—I wanted to dip my feet and hands in the crisp curls of water, to feel its cool touch and the sliding movement of the shingle that scurried with a sharp protesting tinkle after the retreating water.

CHAPTER IV

CORONATION SCENE

FOUR days before my seventh birthday Queen Victoria died. During her last illness while she lingered speechless and apparently insensible, the country awaited with incredulity the end of an epoch. In the words of a later chronicler of the event, 'it appeared as if some monstrous reversal of the course of nature was about to take place.' In August of the following year the coronation of King Edward VII was held. After a period of stunned acquiescence the public mood changed. A new hope and a rising excitement culminated in scenes of revelry and celebration.

In our small town the streets were full of people, bands played, flags and bunting were everywhere displayed.

Across the top of Cornhill House a banner petitioned the Almighty to 'Bless our King and Queen.' Hundreds of fairy lamps in red, white, and blue festooned windows, walls, and the iron trellis-work of the veranda above the shop front.

The arrangement of these fairy lamps had entailed a considerable amount of work and preparation. The fairy lamps themselves, small vases of coloured glass, were procured wholesale. A number were exhibited in the shop window for sale at a penny each. The remainder were used to decorate Cornhill House, and each one of these was fitted out with a small candle made for the purpose.

My parents had promised that I might stay up late on Coronation Day to see the illuminations and to watch the firework display which my father had arranged to take place on our veranda for the benefit of the townspeople.

After tea I awaited impatiently the coming of darkness. Never, it seemed, had the sun set so slowly. It appeared to descend the heavens unwillingly as if reluctant to miss the coming events. I looked out of the front door only to see the teasing reflections of the sun's rays blazing from the windows of the houses on the other side of the square. In the garden the trees flung long shadows across the ground, but above them the air was clear and luminous. Darkness seemed so far off that I found it difficult to imagine what night looked like. Could it be possible that eventually the sharp bright colours of the flowers and the green of the grass would fade into blackness?

A slight chill was in the air and my mother called me indoors. She said that I had better wash my face and hands and brush my hair. I performed these unwelcome duties perfunctorily—too restless to apply myself to any given task. When I came downstairs again to the dining-room my mother discovered that I had broken a boot-lace and that one of my elastic garters needed repair. I fidgeted fretfully while these matters were attended to. My mother was making a final survey of my clothing and general appearance when through the open door I caught sight of my father ascending the stairs, followed by two men carrying step-ladders. Immediately I was off after them. I knew what they were going to do. The realization came to me suddenly. The candles in the fairy lamps would have to be lit while it was still light enough to see.

The trio with me in its wake made its way carefully through the drawing-room, the windows of which gave access to the veranda. My mother had pulled back the carpet and put newspaper on the stained floor to take the dirt. I crawled through this window and stood on the lead roof outside and as I did so was aware of the first shy intimations of approaching twilight. The sky had paled as if somewhere above a few lights had been shut off. The atmosphere had lost its lambency and was faintly veiled.

An hour later it was dark. A crowd filled the market square and the sound of voices rose in a murmur of anticipation. The fairy lamps were now alight; the front of the house had blossomed with luminous petals. The flames of the candles behind the crude coloured glass rose and fell, dimmed to vanishing point only to reappear steady and confident.

Then the fireworks started. Two rockets, hissing like angry snakes, rushed violently into the blackness above. The sound startled me and I gripped the iron balustrade with tense fingers. Below the crowd gave a vast collective sigh that reached its apogee as the rockets burst into clusters of stars which slowly descended trailing long coloured stems behind them.

My father and his assistants now got to work in earnest. Catherine-wheels revolved like flaming sunflowers, fire-balls exploded, and golden rain cascaded in fountains of liquid fire. Paper balloons shaped like parachutes, beneath which lighted wads of cotton wool produced an expansion of air, floated up and up until the tiny flames were lost to view.

Under the spell of movement and colour time flew. All too soon the display came to an end; and fatigue, which excitement had held in check, overwhelmed me. My eyelids drooped, the faces of the crowd, like rows of pale nocturnal flowers, seemed a long way off; they swayed, wavered, and merged together.

Then all at once every one was singing. Song after song was bellowed upon the night air. *Rule,*

Britannia; *Land of Hope and Glory*; *Auld Lang Syne*; *God Save the King*—each sung with ever-increasing frenzy and fervour. The deep-throated roar of sound filled me with apprehension. I could not put my fear into words. I was tired, nervous, and confused. The mass emotion of the crowd, that terrible and implacable force, was like a physical assault upon my nerves. I crouched down upon the window-sill, my hands to my ears, and there my parents found me.

'It's time you were in bed,' said my mother, 'the excitement has been too much for you.'

My father picked me up in his arms and carried me into the house. But I was already asleep.

CHAPTER V

AT THE MEAL TABLE AND MR. TOMKINS

THE assistants employed by my father 'lived in' and shared our table. There were four women assistants and two men, so that every time we sat down there was quite a party. This gave little chance for family or private conversation, and the talk was largely of a business nature with a few remarks about the weather or the health and inclinations of the assistants contributed by my mother, who in addition to being the 'governor's' wife, acted also in the capacity of housekeeper, supervisor, and general mentor to the assistants.

At breakfast my father would deal with his post, which consisted chiefly of invoices of goods due to arrive on that day. From my position at his side I was able to examine the invoices and note their imposing headings. The name of the firm was splashed in large copperplate lettering across the top of the page with scrolls and ornamentation. Very often, and this intrigued me beyond all else, there was a picture of the warehouse itself—an enormous building running down one street and up another, with hundreds of windows, imposing entrances, and a banner fluttering proudly and triumphantly from the roof top. The streets round about were empty except for a horse and van or a single figure hurrying along almost lost against the immensity of the background. Those wide thoroughfares contained nothing so humble as shops or dwellings and served by contrast to present the warehouse as something huge, monstrous, and almost sinister. Its reproduction on the invoice was so large and top-heavy that the items of goods below looked like parallel processions of insects beneath a mountain range.

An entry would catch my father's eye, relating perhaps to a special order anxiously awaited by a customer, and he would say, looking up at one of the 'young ladies,' who took 'first sales' in the department:

'Well, Miss Brown, that O.S. blouse for your customer is invoiced to-day.'

Whereupon Miss Brown, from professional interest or a desire to placate her employer, would express a gratified surprise. Those business references passed and repassed over my head like brilliant-plumaged shuttlecocks. I had no understanding of them, they related to a mysterious world outside my ken; but my imagination gave to them a significance far greater than reality. The term O.S. was totally incomprehensible to me. Sometimes annoyed and irritated by my ignorance, I would suppose it was a joke between my father and the assistant—that O.S. blouse stood for 'old silly blouse' and that the speakers, in spite of their gravity, were being facetious at my expense.

Another word I sometimes heard was fichu (a triangular piece of lace worn by ladies to cover the neck) and this I confused with fissure, a word I had seen, but never tried to pronounce, in the boys' paper the *Marvel*, when Jack, Sam, and Pete, characters in the principal story, had experienced an earthquake, 'and to their horror the earth trembled and gaping fissures appeared on either side of them.'

When my father used this word, saying perhaps, 'Did Mrs. Jones see the fichu when she was in yesterday?' I imagined the 'first sales' waving a wand (which would be the yard-stick which my father carried about with him when he was measuring some part of the house for repairs), and at this gesture I saw in my mind's eye the shop floor cracking suddenly apart before the startled gaze of the innocent customer.

The shop did not close for the midday meal, which necessitated two parties for dinner. My father, who seemed during the working day to be at the beck and call of both customers and assistants, had no set time for his meals and would sometimes begin with the first party and end with the second. Even when he sat down he was still, as it were, attached by some invisible thread to the activities of the shop. Barely had he seated himself and uncovered the plate which my mother had kept hot for him, when an interruption would occur. A knock at the door, to which my father, holding the dish-cover, arrested in mid air, would shout: 'Come in,' and there standing in the doorway would appear one of the 'young ladies.'

'Sign, please,' she would say, and approach my father with her particular problem. 'Miss Robinson would like to take a hat on approval.'

'Do you know her?'

'No, sir, but I think she's all right. She has paid for the vest and petticoat she has just bought.'

'Very well. Tell her we must have it back to-morrow at the latest.'

This conversation, brief and to the point, gave me the feeling that momentous decisions were being made. The words 'Sign, please,' used in the shop by an assistant who wished my father to check and sign a bill, had by custom become the usual formula for every sort of approach; and when it was uttered by the assistant standing in the doorway it sounded to me like a code or password without which it would be impossible to cross the threshold. The sudden and almost peremptory manner in which it was spoken gave it a note of indisputable authority as though at its very sound confidence and security were thereby attained.

I had very little interest in the 'young lady' assistants—they were just a feminine background—but Mr. Tomkins of the men's outfitting department had early attracted my attention. One day as I was wandering about at the top of the house, he opened his bedroom door and I caught sight of a large black box standing on a table.

'What's that?' I inquired, and Mr. Tomkins, noticing the direction of my gaze, at once became very mysterious. He put his finger to his lips to command my silence, looked about him as though he expected to see someone watching us, and then beckoned me into the room. He opened the box and took from it a small wooden cabinet, some strange-looking tumblers, a white silk handkerchief, a piece of black velvet, and an ebony wand. He opened a sliding door in the cabinet and placed the silk handkerchief inside. When he again opened the door the handkerchief had vanished. Presently it reappeared, but this time it was red, white, and blue.

I was intrigued and astounded. Mr. Tomkins was a conjurer and had performed on the stage, but I had never even heard of conjuring, which made Mr. Tomkins's tricks all the more amazing. Mr. Tomkins begged me to keep his secret, which I readily promised to do—though I could see no reason why my father should object to employing a man as an assistant who was also a magician.

I knew Mr. Tomkins was a good assistant, I had heard my father say so. In one respect Mr. Tomkins was lucky—he had succeeded a failure. He had taken the place of a young man who on every count might have been regarded as the perfect salesman. Mr. Venn, for such was his name, was punctual, polite, painstaking, and presentable.   To see him serve a customer was to witness an artist at work.   His voice, clear and articulate, kept up a running commentary: 'A tie, sir? Yes, sir.   How about this one, sir?   The very latest mode, sir—sun-resisting, uncrushable, and even washable, sir.   We run it in all the newest and most select shades, sir.   Made to wear and last, will not slip, slide, bunch, cockle, or crease, sir.'

During this monologue Mr. Venn would dart about with the agility of a squirrel and hold the tie in every conceivable position—on the counter, over his arm, against his collar, and finally high in the air, as though he had come to the conclusion that the tie was a painting and best viewed from a distance.

Unfortunately for Mr. Venn his slick salesmanship was wasted upon the country people for whom my father catered.   The unceasing flow of words, the rushing about, the quick dexterity of Mr. Venn's hands, dazzled and confused them.   They preferred someone who could match their slow, stolid approach, ruminate with them upon the vagaries of the weather, listen sympathetically to their personal problems, and cap their rustic jokes.

One old countryman who was served by the efficient Mr. Venn watched his performance in slow wonderment which finally turned to impatience.   At last he burst out: 'La, zur, thee be all "zur."   My name be Jarge and I likes to be called plain Jarge.'

This was something beyond Mr. Venn, he could not cope with it.   He had every virtue of the salesman except adaptability—and so Mr. Venn had to go and Mr. Tomkins reigned in his stead.

CHAPTER VI

THE FAIR

In October when the nights began to grow chilly, when the days were calm and quiet and the sun shone thinly without warmth—an anaemic reflection of its summer self—when the ground was tangled with dead growth and the leaves fluttered from the trees, when the first bonfire crackled and smoked and sent out sudden leaping tongues of flame, when people began to think of warmer underwear and the new autumn stocks filled the windows of the shop—the fair came to our town.

When I awoke in the mornings, no matter how early, I heard the sound of activity in the market square; the thud of hammers, the shouts of men, the snorting of traction engines, the heavy movement of trucks. And when I looked out of the window I saw a skeleton framework rising foot by foot, mounting up in the dim dawn light, expanding and growing and becoming minute by minute more solid, more recognizable, until eventually when morning had come and gone the fair had become a solid construction of assembled roundabouts; switchbacks; imposing - fronted side-shows—gilded, lamplit, displaying painted pictures of lions, tigers, dancing women, and dwarfs; stalls filled to overflowing with nougat, brandy-snaps, and confetti; coco-nut shies; and the tall, elongated, bell-surmounted, try-your-strength machines; and in odd corners, tucked away behind the larger erections, or beneath the rising platform of the curving switchback, the tiny booths of the fortune-teller, the palmist, and the phrenologist.

Hurrying home from school at midday I snatched a hasty meal and then ran out into the square to watch the final activities before the fair commenced. The painted wooden horses were lifted from their wagons and bolted into position upon the roundabouts; the cars of the switchback sped up and down upon a trial run, musical organs were tested and emitted sudden sharp bursts of brazen sound; groups of men clinging to the bright rainbow-coloured roofs fitted gaily coloured lengths of wood into their appointed sockets.

Engrossed, fascinated, I lost all count of time until looking up at the town hall clock, now almost hidden from view behind the striped awnings of the fair, I saw the large hand almost at the vertical, and reluctantly yet dutifully I turned away to rush panting and breathless to make a late entry to afternoon school.

It was when darkness fell that the fair came fully into its own. A transformation took place—nature, as though determined to take a hand, blacked out the shuttered shops and houses of the market square so that against the darkened background the lights of the fair became a brilliant swirling kaleidoscope. The brassy roar of steam-driven organs blared at their loudest pitch; a medley of tunes produced a wild intoxicating punch-bowl of drunken sound. Above the revolving coloured lamps of the switchback the plump arc lamps hissed and spluttered like fussy, pompous old gentlemen shocked at the scene displayed by their own illumination. The fair whirled to a mounting crescendo of frenzy. Rides on the roundabouts became faster and shorter; girls clad in tights danced with twinkling legs upon the platforms outside the side-shows; men in wrinkled and grease-stained evening dress waved top-hats in mute appealing gestures of invitation to see the wonders enacted within

the interiors of canvas auditoriums; voices bawled,
bells were rung; and even the vendors of the small
stalls, standing beneath their oil lamps, raised their
voices hoarsely as though they too were caught up in
the collective excitement. Beneath all these noises
was a throbbing undercurrent of sound—the deep
pulsation of the electric dynamos driven by the
driving belts of the high and massive traction engines.

Every year by dint of great effort I managed to
save ninepence to spend at the fair. To this my
father contributed an additional sixpence, and when this
was gone my mother could be relied upon for another
modest sum, so that altogether I deemed myself
wealthy and was able to indulge in that most delightful
of all moods, the feeling of blind, wilful, reckless
extravagance. But I did not spend my money
immediately. The fair ran for three days and there
was much to see without the expenditure of a single
penny. At first I husbanded the contents of my
purse, enjoying the delights of anticipation and thus
enhancing the ecstasy of the final fling. I drifted
round with the crowds, carried along by their mass
weight willy-nilly in whatsoever direction they might
move. I saw the fat woman smirking obesely
from her throne-like chair; I watched the sword
swallower lower his glinting rapier of steel into his
insides, marvelled at the black man dancing with
naked feet upon sizzling red-hot iron bars; joined a
group which grinned sheepishly at the antics of the
performing bear; witnessed muscle-armed men swing
the heavy hammer that sent the sliding disk shooting
up the tall wooden frame of the try-your-strength
machine—sometimes to reach the top and ring the bell.
When I did spend my money, most of it went on
the switchback. Once or twice I rode on the 'gal-

loping horses,' but this form of amusement had little appeal for me; it was tame sitting on a wooden horse and jogging up and down, round and round, clinging to a spiral brass bar which seemed to revolve in my hands.

But the switchback was different: you sat on a red velvet seat and put your feet up on the rail in front, felt the heavy car gather speed and go rolling weightily up the slopes so that your back was pressed snugly against the back of the seat, up and over and down the other side with all your weight now on your feet —while overhead the great yellow globes of light dipped and rose, rose and dipped, matching the ascent and descent of the cars—and below and in front of you the foremost cars raced ahead and the gilded bars that connected them twisted and gleamed like fat sticks of golden sugar-cane.

It was not only the ride which fascinated me—the sensuous feeling of gliding through the air, with the shops and houses and the faces of the people below merging to form a bizarre arabesque pattern as though I was enclosed within a crazy quilt of exotic design—but I was intrigued too by the mechanical and business side of the switchback.

When I turned my head away from the tilting background of the market square, and looked at the centre of this revolving mechanism, I saw the squat tubby belly of the steam engine which supplied the power to keep us in motion. And down below on the coal-strewn floor was a table which constituted the 'box office' and behind which was seated an enormous woman. This custodian of the purse piled the receipts in open array upon the table-top. Black columns of pennies and halfpennies stood side by side against the lighter-hued piles of silver and even gold.

As my car swung down opposite this treasury table

the dark, greasy collector of our fares jumped nimbly
from the running-board and handed his quota of
money to the sphinx-faced female receptionist who,
with practised skill, transferred it to the growing
columns of coin on the table before her.   In the cold
light of the arc lamps I saw the sparkle of stones from
the rings on her fingers as her hands darted backwards and forwards ceaselessly sifting, counting,
arranging, and apportioning her precious counters.

This was a 'back-stage' view of the switchback,
but the 'front of the house' on the other side claimed
the most attention.   Here, facing the steps by which
patrons ascended to the elevated platform, were to be
seen the gilt pipes of the organ itself, from the slotted
mouths of which as we rolled majestically before them
we received the full frantic belch of the whiny music.

When, as sometimes happened, my car stopped on
this side—as though unnerved and rendered immobile
by the sheer density and spate of sound—I was able
to watch the diminutive animated figures which
decorated the front of the organ.   The heads of
these manikins jerked from side to side in a constant
St. Vitus's dance, while with their hands they beat with
hammers upon small bells, producing a tiny tin-
tinnabulation scarcely to be heard against the musical
thunder which rolled about them.

Situated on the outskirts of the fair small stalls
competed in games of skill and chance.   In dim
corners, lit only by a couple of evil-smelling naphtha
oil lamps which hissed and flared sending out thin
horizontal points of flame like the luminous fangs of
some fabulous reptile, these stalls had about them an
atmosphere of shabby illegality which the surly mien
and swarthy countenances of their proprietors did
little to dispel.

One such stall displayed a small wooden platform which supported two uprights joined by a cross-bar. From the centre of the cross-bar, suspended by a length of cord, hung a wooden ball. Almost immediately behind the ball stood a ninepin. To gain a prize (half a crown, or one of the many watches and clocks which lined the shelves at the back of the stall in massed ticking array) it was necessary to swing the ball forward and knock over the ninepin in reverse— that is to say from behind. It looked simple, but the ball on being swung to the right or left in order to clear the ninepin on the forward swing inevitably circled the object instead of hitting it when it swung back.

Now it so happened that in our dining-room at home there hung over one end of the table a bell-push which my mother used to communicate with the kitchen (one ring, bring in the sweets—two rings, clear away).

This, I thought, as I stood puzzled before the fair stall, would make an excellent substitute for practice. The next day I fixed up a box on the table and stood a ninepin behind the bell-push. I tried swinging the bell-push at every conceivable angle until I could hit the ninepin over from the rear with ease. That evening I went up to the stall in the fair to try conclusions with the real thing. The fair man took my twopence with a smile of condescension. Another mug and a young 'un this time, he doubtless thought. I thought so too. I had no expectation of success. I swung the ball at the angle at which I had practised and down went the ninepin. The onlookers murmured approval and the stall-keeper made the best of a bad job. Handing me a gun-metal watch he shouted: 'There you are, folks, see how easy it is— even a boy can do it.'

CHAPTER VII

EARLY EXPERIENCES

At school I made friends with a boy who had an insatiable curiosity about the human anatomy and told me many horrible stories of strange diseases which he claimed afflicted the flesh of man. He asserted that under certain conditions the human backside was liable to shrink and wither. I was so alarmed at this disclosure that I endeavoured at once to obtain a view of my own posterior, but as there was no mirror in my bedroom I was obliged to give up the attempt and hope for the best.

I may remark here that neither at that time nor for many years later had I any but the vaguest ideas about sex; and what was perhaps more strange, had never to my knowledge heard a swear word and would not have recognized one had I seen it printed or heard it spoken.

Once glancing through a book belonging to my father I saw a word printed d——d, but regarded it as a misprint. My father, always abreast with the times, had recently purchased a typewriter, an original Remington model of early pattern. Idly tapping away with one finger on this high, cumbersome machine, I inadvertently tapped out a dash instead of a letter. Then when I came upon the word d——d in the book I imagined that the printer in setting up the type had made a similar mistake.

This ignorance of swearing proved on one occasion an embarrassment. I had taken a note for my mother to a distant and less familiar part of the town and had nearly reached my destination when I was accosted by a group of loutish youths. Their leader seized my arm and addressed me as 'little velvet pants.' As I was wearing not velvet but good sensible tweed, I took this remark as ill-merited and attempted to break away. At which another of the gang seized my free arm and emulating his leader gave it a decided twist.

'What shall we do with 'un?' said one.

'Let's make 'un swear,' said another. 'Eh, that be a good idea.'

And scowling ferociously into my face, the leader said:

'Go on, velvet pants, let's 'ear thee cuss a bit.'

Not knowing what to say, I remained silent, which was naturally attributed to stubbornness and ill will on my part. Baffled but not defeated, the leader gave my arm a more vicious twist accompanied by a knowing leer.

'Come on, baby pants, say these 'ere words after me and we'll let 'ee go.'

At this moment there appeared round the corner of the street the figure of a policeman. The youths bolted and my education in the language of oaths came to an abrupt termination.

My mother was very anxious that I should learn to play the piano. She did not require any very high standard of proficiency; it would be enough, she said, if I could play a few simple tunes, or a hymn like *Onward, Christian Soldiers.*

In this I was to disappoint her, for I had no ear for music and my small hands were clumsy and inelastic at the keys. However, the attempt was made and regularly every Friday I spent an hour with my instructor—a Miss Kemp, whose front door bore a brass plate with the simple unadorned inscription 'Music Teacher.'

*B

This hour was for me such drudgery that the day took its place in my mind as Black Friday. There was, however, one compensation—Friday was the day I received my pocket-money—a coincidence, I fancy, that my mother had cunningly contrived. My pocket-money was twopence a week, a penny of which I was persuaded to save. The necessity for thrift was constantly impressed upon me by my mother, who told me tragic stories of improvidence in which the word 'bankrupt' frequently appeared. I had no idea of the meaning of the word, but my mother's serious countenance and the horror in her voice as she uttered this word left me in no doubt that it related to something terrible and irrevocable, like being cast into a bottomless pit or caught on the prongs of the devil's trident.

On the way to my music lesson I would loiter with intent to spend my penny. I had no foolish ideas of business first—the things I bought would be in my pocket to comfort me through the coming ordeal. First I called at a newsagent's and spent a halfpenny on the boys' paper the *Marvel*, which contained each week a story of the exploits of 'Stanley Dare, the boy detective.' Later this paper was enlarged to include an additional story of the adventures of Jack, Sam, and Pete. My next stop was next door to the music teacher's house, where an enterprising carpenter employed a lathe turning out hundreds of wooden spinning-tops. Though the cost of a top was only a halfpenny, its choice was a matter of long and solemn conjecture. There were 'sweet' tops and 'bad' tops. A sweet top under the skilful lash of the whip would spin rhythmically and with honest pride, but a bad top would without warning take a sudden and disconcerting leap into the air and was known among experienced practitioners as a 'window breaker.'

While the *Marvel* was a constant purchase, I did not always, of course, buy a top with the remaining halfpenny. During perhaps three weeks out of four this went on sweets. My favourite choice, judged by quantity rather than quality, was liquorice allsorts —which were sold at four ounces a penny. It must have been sheer greed which prompted me to buy them, for I had no great love for the taste of liquorice —it reminded me too closely of a black liquorice draught which my mother gave me when I was 'out of sorts.'

The shop which sold these sweets was kept by an old woman whose sight was badly failing her. Her wares were kept in large open boxes placed in a row on the counter, and unscrupulous boys, aware of her partial blindness, would sometimes snatch a handful of sweets without payment. As a counter-attack to these methods, the old lady carried always a stout cane with which she whacked the boxes at regular intervals. This she did from the moment a boy entered the shop until the time he left—thus safeguarding her stock against all and sundry, since she reposed no trust in either friend or foe.

When I first entered the shop I found this procedure somewhat startling, but what I most disliked about the shop was the smell. The old lady cooked and displayed in the window meat faggots and black-puddings —strange-looking balls of suet and mincemeat which might perhaps be described as bastard descendants of the haggis family. On a hot summer day the interior of the shop held an atmosphere that was almost overwhelming, but fortunately the liquorice allsorts remained untainted—a fact which upon closer inspection may be deemed to hold a moral.

The market square was full of interesting shops.

Quite close to where we lived was a small grocer's kept by two bachelor brothers—Mr. Charles and Mr. Benjamin Brown. They were twins, both very short and active. I had a difficulty in distinguishing one from the other, but presently grew to recognize Mr. Charles by his smile—for Mr. Benjamin never allowed himself this indulgence. He was in fact a suspicious man and it was my delight to see him ring a half-sovereign on the counter in order to make sure that it was genuine. This he did with great intensity and concentration, his forehead creased in a frown, his head held sideways; one could almost imagine his ear twitching with apprehension. He was quite un-self-conscious in the matter, with apparently no idea that this pantomime might strike his customer as ludicrous or even insulting.

The grocer's shop front consisted of two bow windows between which three steps led to the front door. On either side of the steps, beneath the windows, were hung straw baskets of the kind that are used by carpenters for carrying their tools. Two or three times a day Mr. Benjamin would make a thorough examination of the baskets. Emerging rapidly from the shop and standing exactly opposite the steps, he would first view the baskets from an upright position, obtaining as it were a sort of general perspective. Then approaching nearer and bending down with his hands on his knees until his eyes were on a level with the baskets, he would peer first at the two that hung on the right-hand side and then at the two on the left-hand side. The sight of the little man squatting on his heels afforded my parents and me regular amusement.

'Quick!' my mother would call. 'Mr. Benjamin is examining his baskets,' and I would run to the window to see the grocer go through his routine.

We often discussed the possible reason for this examination. Was he counting them to make sure that they were still there, or did his meticulous mind insist upon a perfect alignment? Our conjectures remained unanswered and the mystery unsolved.

My pocket-money was eventually increased to four-pence a week. Of this sum I still dutifully saved a penny which when deposited in my money-box became an irre-vocable gift to fortune, for the box was strongly made and had no opening other than a small slot at the top protected by a concealed spring which prevented the unorthodox extraction of coins with the blade of a knife.

I was now able to buy other papers in addition to the *Marvel*. New ones had recently appeared, each in their different ways equally appealing. There was the *Boys' Friend* on pale green paper, the *Boys' Herald* on white, and the *Boys' Realm* on pink. The stories in the *Boys' Friend* were well mixed, the *Boys' Herald* was strong in adventure yarns, and the *Boys' Realm* had a special exotic atmosphere all its own, with fantastic stories of inventions, strange worlds, and fabulous people.

In the *Boys' Friend* there was a serial story about a reformed drunkard who set off on a voyage of explora-tion across the desert with a water-bottle at his hip instead of his usual flask of whisky. I remember this story because it aroused my father's interest and I persuaded him to read it aloud to me week by week. This was an innovation, for although my father had been in the habit of reading to me on Sundays, the books chosen were usually *Don Quixote*, or the plays of Shakespeare. My father was a great lover of Shakespeare and had presented me with a complete volume of the poet's plays in microscopic type dedicated to 'Norman Hancock on his attaining the age of

50 days,' an attainment he evidently regarded as a matter worthy of celebration.

In addition to the Shakespeare I possessed a copy of Longfellow's poems (unread). Apart from these two classics (hateful and pretentious word) my remaining books, judged as literature, showed a sharp decline in matter and style. My mother had taken in *Home Chat* for a number of years and the supplement for children, entitled 'The Play Box,' containing the adventures of 'Jungle Jinks,' was detached and given to me. Several hundreds of these supplements had been bound to form (at least judging from its outward appearance) an imposing volume. The remainder of my library consisted of *Sons of the Empire*, a book of stories for boys (from the shop stock, 1s. 11¾d.), a bound volume of the halfpenny *Marvel*, some copies of 'Books for the Bairns,' including Kingsley's *Heroes* and the adventures of *Brer Rabbit*, and a paper-covered edition of *Helen's Babies*.

This last book had been given to me by an aunt, much to my disgust, for a title which included the word 'baby' seemed to me a gratuitous insult. However, one wet afternoon, having nothing better to do, I started to read it. It is the story of a bachelor left in charge of two difficult children. All I can remember about it now is the persistent cry of the younger child: 'Want to see the wheels go round,' when shown the gentleman's watch. I liked to see wheels go round myself, so that this part of the book seemed thoroughly sensible, but after this incident my interest waned and I left the book unfinished.

Later another book came into my possession, namely *Eric, or Little by Little* by Dean Farrar, the sub-title of which incidentally was an accurate description of the growth of my library. This book was my first school prize. The word prize is rather inaccurate, for honesty compels me to admit that the book was presented not only to myself, but also to every other pupil in the school to commemorate the school's twenty-first anniversary. The gift pleased boys and parents alike and my mother in particular because Dean Farrar was dean of Canterbury, the city in which my mother had spent her childhood.

We were not at that time a bookish family. I had neither opportunity nor inducement to read books. There was no public library in the town and at school very little was taught us about English literature. My mind was slow in growth, I was too young to appreciate the finer writing, and because my mind was not dulled or confused by an attempt to digest work that was too tough for it, I came to maturity without any preconceived ideas about famous writers, and was free to judge their work with an open mind. By an open mind I mean a mind uninfluenced by those literary generalities, conventions, and simplifications which school teachers and popular educators are sometimes apt to propound, with the result that when we hear the name Dickens we think of *Pickwick Papers* and social reform, while we associate De Quincey with an opium pipe, Wordsworth with nature, Keats with beauty, Blake with visions, Shelley with a skylark, and regard Bunyan and Cervantes as men who lived most of their lives in prison.

Fortunately, too, I was never compelled at school to learn passages from the poets by heart, a proceeding which effectively dims, dulls, and even kills the freshness and beauty of poetic expressions and causes the pupil in later years to turn from great work in disgust and revulsion. If it be thought necessary to improve a child's memory by learning by rote let him practise on such authors as Bradshaw, who will at least enable him to catch a train even though he never catch an inspiration.

CHAPTER VIII

GOING OUT TO TEA

My parents soon made friends in the town of our adoption and we received many invitations out to tea.

From my point of view, going out to tea had drawbacks as well as advantages. On the credit side were the piles of good things to eat and the possibility of being able to stay up later than usual. On the debit side there was the necessity of being polite and on one's best behaviour. The tools of the table—knife, spoon, and fork—must be used correctly, elbows must be held close to the side of the body while eating. One could not sniff, brush the hand across the mouth, smack the lips over a particularly delicious mouthful, slouch in the chair, take the best cake on the plate, interrupt adult conversation, or omit to say 'Yes, please,' and 'No, thank you.' If there were other children in the house I was told to go and play with them, and since children have no false modesty regarding the treatment of guests of their own age, this usually meant that I must conform willingly and without question to the desires and requirements of my young hosts. If the game chosen was 'police and robbers' it was I who must be the robber and receive the severe penalties my crime entailed, or if we played at 'war' I would be the cowardly enemy. On the other hand I was never allowed to be a highwayman or a master criminal; both these characters belonged to the 'hero' class. Constant practice in my allotted role enabled me to acquire such proficiency in avoiding capture and punishment that I began to enjoy the employment of my powers. Eventually I turned the tables on my companions by always volunteering for the despised part, which as a result of my agile performance became a much-coveted role.

Some of the houses we visited were without children. At the Brockets', for instance, there were only elderly people. These were the two Miss Brockets, both looking very much alike in their purple silk gowns, their round smiling faces—small, smooth, and unlined beneath abundant hair piled high upon the head. Their brother, Mr. Timothy Brocket, was almost bald, but his small gnome-like features had the same ageless quality. The Brockets seemed never to grow any older, but to remain always the same indeterminate age, as though at some period in their lives time had forgotten them and passed them by.

Tea was taken in the front room—a large shadowy room full of ponderous furniture and massive gilt-framed pictures of dim and sombre landscapes. On the veined marble mantelpiece stood an ornate clock, encased within a glass dome, which muted the sound of its mechanism and reduced its decorous tick to a minute, almost soundless pulse. This room, like the Brockets themselves, had a changeless quality; it would, one felt, endure for all time unaffected by the turbulence of the outer world.

The tea-table glittered with silver ware which caught and reflected the light from the fire—for I associate the room with the steel-grey days of winter —and no lamp was lit while a semblance of daylight remained. We sat in twilight watching the window slowly darken until the firelight gained ascendancy and shadows jumped from face to face, mounted the walls, finally to converge in flickering confusion upon the lofty ceiling.

There were good things to eat for tea. Always a large lard cake (known locally as 'lardy cake'), chocolate biscuits, and, a favourite of mine, thin crisp brandy-snaps, which I saw seldom except on stalls at the fair. It was at the Brockets' that I first tasted anchovy relish. When I saw the round flat china pot I thought it must contain some sort of ointment which had found its way to the table by mistake.

After tea had been eaten and the tea things cleared away the curtains were drawn, and with great care Mr. Timothy placed a heavy oil lamp in the centre of the table, the mahogany surface of which was now covered with a red chenille cloth.

The grown-ups gathered round the fire and I sat on a stool in a corner of the room beside a high cupboard stacked with magazines mostly of a semi-religious nature. I was allowed to open the doors of this cupboard and rummage through its contents. The magazines contained long serial stories by Silas K. Hocking which were depressingly dramatic in style. I read bits here and there and grew pensive and melancholy. When the time arrived for our departure my mind was half dazed by sorrowful fictitious encounters, and the cold moon-swept street into which I emerged seemed part of the stories' unreality.

The house of Mrs. Arnold was in total contrast to the Brockets'. It stood, or rather perhaps one might say it sprawled, elegantly on an embankment above the town. It had an air of lightness and grace. There was a great deal of white paint in the rooms and chairs and sofas were sprightly beneath their coverings of pastel-coloured chintz. The walls were covered with Morris wallpapers and decorated with copies of Pre-Raphaelite paintings depicting knights in armour and slim, willowy maidens dressed in long flowing robes, their faces bunched together in close proximity in a decorative manner, so that they looked rather like a posy of wide-petalled flowers.

Mrs. Arnold was a widow and had something of the cool grace and slender distinction of her pictures. Her speech was refined and contained many dainty euphemisms. She did not ask me if I wished to use the w.c., but said: 'Would the little boy like to wash his hands?' This question occurred with such regularity that I gained the impression that she had an exceptional regard for personal cleanliness.

Mrs. Arnold was a Liberal in politics, which our Conservative neighbours regarded as an eccentricity. Such an outlook was too unusual to be taken seriously and if it was noticed at all, it was not dwelt upon. Politeness demanded that it should be overlooked like a physical defect.

She had a great admiration for Mr. Gladstone and would often refer to him as the 'Grand Old Man.' I had no idea who this grand old man could be. I thought of him as having a much-lined and kindly face. Possibly he was a friend of Mrs. Arnold's and it might be that I would eventually meet him, for so frequently did Mrs. Arnold speak of him that I did not realize he was dead.

The tea-table was arranged very daintily with mats and lace doilies beneath the thin cups and saucers. There were home-made bread and cakes to eat and a good deal of fruit. In fact the centre-piece was almost invariably a large pineapple placed in a vertical position on a tall silver dish. When I looked at it I used to imagine it was a fruitarian model of a Jules Verne invention—a rocket perhaps just about to take off into the stratosphere.

The deep recesses of Mrs. Arnold's white bookshelves contained a number of Victorian illustrated books, *The Parables of Our Lord*, illustrated by J. E. Millais, Dalziel's *Arabian Nights*, Birket Foster's *English Landscape*, the illustrated Tennyson of 1857, and many others.

The *Arabian Nights* was my favourite and I would become engrossed in the pictures, quite unaware of the incongruity between the Eastern settings and the figures of the women, who were dressed in the voluminous clothing usually associated with English ladies of the mid-Victorian era.

The famous engraving by Rossetti illustrating Tennyson's *Palace of Art* also held a fascination for me even though I did not understand it. What was the curious instrument the woman was playing? Why was it placed on top of a dungeon and who was the man—half human, half angel—bending over her?

Even the minor details of the engraving were entrancing and there were so many of them—ships on the sea, a walled harbour, a fort, men firing a cannon on the battlements, an archer in the court-yard, a sun-dial, and in the foreground a soldier nonchalantly munching an apple.

Through this picture, like Alice through the looking-glass, I entered into a fairy world of my own making.

CHAPTER IX

AUNT MARTHA
AND SOME STREET ADVENTURES

SOMETIMES my Aunt Martha, my mother's sister, came to stay with us from Kent. Living with her brother and his wife she was kept busy with house-work and the care of the children, so that a holiday with us was not only a rare event, but also a rest which she immensely enjoyed.

She was small and dumpy in figure with small, plump hands. Her podgy Queen-Victorian face showed a serene contentment, belied only by weak protuberant eyes which bulged uncertainly upon the world as though a little frightened and uncertain of their possible reception. She wore dark rather form-less dresses edged at the neck with a pointed white collar, and although she suffered from swollen ankles she persisted in the choice of small-fitting, elegant shoes.

Simple, credulous, soft-hearted, emotional, and entirely free from egotism, she was popular and well received in the company of others; her innocuous remarks kept the conversation free of entanglement, her gossip held no venom, and her innocent delight in the small-talk of her friends made her a favourite at tea parties and social gatherings.

During her stay she would help my mother with her needlework and her presence as she sat at her sewing gave to the room an atmosphere of tranquillity, a feeling still further enhanced by her bright, simple remarks delivered in a soft, almost childish voice, which seemed to impregnate the air with the very essence of the comfortable and familiar.

As the evenings drew in and darkness fell Aunt Martha took up a position by the fireplace with her feet resting on a hassock.   Presently she would lay aside her work and say to my mother, who was perhaps cleaning out a cupboard or covering jam: 'Must give up now, m'dear, eyes are getting tired.'   Then she would put a handkerchief over her face and take 'forty winks' or if wakeful sit motionless, her eyes on my father as he sat at the table checking his invoices. And there would be silence in the room, broken only by the sound of the gas popping against a broken mantle, the sibilant whisper of my father's voice as he muttered over a column of figures, and the movements of my mother from table to cupboard.   This silence was maintained in order that my father should be undisturbed, but sometimes a remark would be exchanged between Aunt Martha and my mother, leading to a short snatch of conversation.   Then, as though aware of the seated figure bending over the papers on the table, the conversation would cease abruptly like a small wind that rises suddenly and as suddenly dies away.

When the weather was favourable my mother would arrange to take Aunt Martha for a drive through the countryside in an open landau.   The landau was a four-wheel carriage with a top in two parts, so that it might be closed or thrown half or entirely open. Our carriage was hired from a Mr. Enright, who was both proprietor and driver.   Mr. Enright was noted for his careful driving, a very important factor in the estimation of the ladies who employed him.   During the summer months he was in great demand and it was necessary to book him well ahead.

Before Mr. Enright arrived at our house my mother and Aunt Martha put in a great deal of preparation for the excursion. If the weather was hot, parasols and long white gloves were brought out; if the sky was overcast, discussion centred on the choice of raincoats and rugs. I generally accompanied the ladies on these occasions and was told to hold myself in readiness so that I might be made 'presentable.' This meant that I must stay close at hand and not go out in the garden or be in any place where it would be difficult to find me at a moment's notice. In the meantime my mother would be hovering about giving last-minute orders to cook about the tea for my father and the assistants and making every arrangement for the smooth working of the domestic machine during her absence. Then before she went up to her room to change, she would 'get me ready'—a portmanteau phrase which included a number of activities such as washing, brushing my hair, cleaning teeth and nails, putting on my best suit, and the pulling up of socks which, to employ a barometrical term, were usually at 'stormy.' Finally when all this had been done to my mother's satisfaction, I was posted at the window to announce the arrival of the landau.

Precisely at the appointed time Mr. Enright drove up, and after applying the brakes and depositing his whip in its holder, he folded his arms and sat in solemn dignity as if to say: 'Behold, the hour has struck and I am here.' On no account would Mr. Enright announce himself by such an obvious method as hammering a knocker or ringing a door-bell. To him time was time and one had only to glance at a reliable clock to be assured of the moment of his arrival. Alas for this precept of punctuality, the clock was always fast as far as the ladies were concerned. Aunt Martha was the principal offender. Meticulous in dressing she was determined to do credit to the occasion, and Mr. Enright's arrival invariably coincided with the moment when she was making her choice of ear-rings and brooches.

My mother, becoming impatient, would call out: 'Martha, Martha, are you ready?' and my aunt's muffled voice would be heard in reply: 'Just coming, m'dear, can't find my cameo brooch.' Eventually she would emerge red in the face from her sartorial exertions, to join us at the foot of the stairs. Even then she was not completely ready. She would push and pat at brooch and ear-rings and squint at various ornaments that occupied points on her person almost out of range of her vision. During this difficult operation she apologized for her delay in tremulous, almost tearful accents.

When finally we all three appeared rather self-consciously on the pavement Mr. Enright with great gallantry jumped down, touched his hat, and opened the carriage door for the ladies to enter. Off we went bowling along at a steady pace. At intervals Mr. Enright cracked his whip, which made a noise like a pistol shot. This accomplishment had no effect whatever upon the horse, which neither blinked nor altered its gait. No doubt it had long accepted Mr. Enright's performance for what it was—a gesture of professional pride.

Our route lay in the direction of the railway station and on the way we overtook the town omnibus which ran to and fro to meet the principal trains. My mother recognized some people in the bus and as we drove alongside she smiled and bowed to them. The people behind the thick glass windows of the omnibus smiled back—their mouths opening without sound like the mouths of fish in an aquarium. I felt a snobbish pride at the idea of riding in a private carriage, while those less fortunate people were obliged to share a public conveyance. Moreover, I had a personal grudge against this particular omnibus. At school I had been dared to jump on the step at the rear of the bus and so obtain a free ride to the station. Hanging on to the back of a vehicle for a ride was much practised by boys before the advent of the motor-car, and was known as a 'whip-behind,' so called because other boys on catching sight of the hanger-on would out of mischief or malice shout out to the driver: 'Whip behind you, mister!' When I took on my dare and mounted the steps of the omnibus, a perfect chorus of 'Whip-behinds' rent the air. The fact was I had ill judged the time for my adventure. I had chosen the very moment when the bus passed the elementary school, and scores of boys surging through the gates on their way home glee-fully took up the cry.

The bus driver, a kindly man, could not ignore this clamour and was obliged out of self-respect to crack his whip. Actually I was well out of range, but the very fact of discovery was enough to frighten me and I attempted to make a skilful jump to the ground while the vehicle was in motion. The position of the step and the width of the bus prevented my jumping forward and so overcoming or at least reducing my momentum, and moreover the bus was trundling downhill at a good speed. Thus when I jumped I hit the ground with a force that half stunned me and sent me tumbling into the gutter. Whereat a cheer went up from the watching crowd of boys and I became, in spite of my bedraggled appearance, a temporary hero. And such is the unreason of the mind and the clannish spirit of youth, that I blamed the driver of the bus for my misfortune rather than the boys who had cried out and betrayed me.

When I remember that drive through the leafy

Somerset lanes I experience a certain nostalgia. The dust and grit of the road and the musty smell that emanated from the carriage covers, squashed like a concertina behind us, have in retrospect endearing qualities. But in point of fact I was not altogether happy on those excursions. The shameful secret must out——I was scared of horses. They seemed to me uncanny creatures, unpredictable in mood and temper. In spite of their apparent subservience to man I had the feeling that they were really his superiors and only awaited an opportunity to prove it in some terrible and audacious act.

One day when I was out with a school friend we narrowly escaped being knocked down by a runaway horse. We were making our way to the railway station, acting on information received from boys at school that the slot-machine at the station was out of order and that for the expenditure of a penny it was possible to pull out the drawer six times, thus obtaining half a dozen bars of chocolate cream for the price of one. Some there were among us who asserted that this was an understatement; they even maintained that once a penny had been inserted in the slot there was no limit to the generosity of this obliging machine, and drawer-pulling could be continued at will. This report, however, was regarded by the more sober-minded as Utopian, while others put a sinister and cynical interpretation upon it. They said that the story of the machine's unlimited dispensations was a deliberate canard calculated to destroy our faith and to give the impression that the whole thing was a hoax, and thus leave a free field for certain interested parties.

However, my friend and I were determined to make a full investigation. After all, even if our hopes were disappointed, we could always fall back on a secondary diversion, namely the putting of halfpennies on the railway line. When the wheels of a train had run over them they were flattened out to the size of a penny, and in spite of their lack of weight such enlarged coins had been known to deceive the mechanism of even the most honourable slot-machine.

The railway station was a mile from the town, and on the day we set out the weather was close and humid. Trudging along beneath a darkening sky we were soon sweating freely, and on our arrival at a point where the road was under repair we took a rest to watch the ponderous movements of a steam-roller. We were standing with our backs to a wall when suddenly a vivid flash of lightning cleft the darkness of the clouds and thunder bellowed across the skies. Rain descended in sheets and we were just about to run for cover when a horse and wagonette came tearing down the road at breakneck speed. It was obvious that the horse was out of control. The reins dragged along the ground and the figure of a man could be seen clinging to the sides of the vehicle. The horse, confronted by the massive bulk of the steam-roller, swerved violently in our direction and the wheels of the swaying wagonette rattled past us with barely an inch or so to spare. Two of the roadmen sprang at the horse's head and, gripping the harness, brought the animal to a trembling standstill.

The shock of this experience put all thoughts of the station out of our heads and, wet and shaken, we returned dejectedly homewards. The gift-giving machine was forgotten. We had now to think of a suitable excuse to explain our rain-drenched garments and to account for the dollops of mud which the wheels of the wagonette had showered upon us.

I do not regret those adventures in street and

roadway; they were a spice to homely routine and brought a zest to life. I can hear some fastidious and circumspect moralist say: 'Fancy playing in the streets!' Well, I loved my garden and knew every inch of it, but the streets represented the unknown—they were mysterious, enticing, delightful. In them anything might happen — and sometimes did. There was always something fresh to explore and discover—an alleyway, a new path, a courtyard, or an unexpected turning. Playing in the streets we learnt many things: the easiest lamp-post to climb and how to make the lamp-lighter fall off his bike; how to walk on the wall that bordered the churchyard, and how to distract the vicar's attention; the size of rain puddles and the sky patterns reflected in them, and how far up over our boots the water would go without seeping in; and on the pavements we learnt the mysteries of hop-scotch; the best place to spin a top; and best of all how to drop a 'dropper,' a hollow tube attached to a string which when dashed to the ground caused a cap to explode with a loud report, much to the annoyance of the people who were often just in front of it.

We learnt too the joys of 'gang' fights; how to stalk and hide from the enemy, or make a dash for cover round pillars and posts or through dim echoing avenues. When the shadows of the houses lengthened we knew the movement of time, and in the refraction of light beneath ragged clouds, and in the changing hues of brick and stone, we knew the beauty of colour.

CHAPTER X

THE BIG FIRE

EVERY summer a carnival was held in the town, the main feature of which was a procession through the streets. The one that I remember best was connected with the 'big shirt.'

The procession included not only soldiers, police, and members of the volunteer fire brigade, but also decorated floats and tradesmen's carts advertising their different wares—and on this occasion the local shirt factory had produced an enormous shirt which, suspended on a wooden framework, was carried through the streets on a cart drawn by a team of white horses. The shirt was so large that the sleeves almost touched the houses on either side as it moved majestically through the ranks of the assembled by-standers, while its collar band was level with the roof-tops. Such a shirt might have been made for a Brobdingnagian. One felt that its size and splendour would bring hope and joy even to Bunyan's Giant Despair.

I was in the garden when the fire at the factory started. The carnival had been concluded during a week of blazing sunshine, and now a few days later the town had relapsed into its usual state of summer somnolence. School holidays were nearly over and I was idly pottering about turning over large stones and pieces of decaying wood and watching the insects —ants, spiders, and wood-lice which I had disturbed in their dark hiding-places. They ran about in a haphazard manner, confused by the glare of the sunlight.

I heard a crackling noise, as though someone was rapidly breaking up a number of dry beansticks. I looked up and saw some smoke puff out from a window at the far end of the shirt factory. There was a sharp tinkle of falling glass and a tongue of flame danced on the roof of the factory. It swayed to and fro like a caterpillar that has come to the end of a log and rears its body in the air blindly groping for support. Then the flame fell down and began to crawl along the gutter. There was a rumbling sound inside the building, which seemed to be suffering from some internal disorder, and then another and larger ball of smoke was belched out of the window.

At first I just stood and gazed in surprised wonderment, then I ran into the house. My mother was talking to cook in the passage. I heard them say that a shirt had caught fire in the factory's airing-room. Immediately I pictured the giant shirt of the carnival waving flaming arms and dancing and nodding like the little flame I had seen on the roof. I asked my mother if I might go out on the pavement, but she said: 'No, you can go in the shop, if you like, and look out of the window.' Then I knew that something very unusual indeed was happening, for I was seldom allowed in the shop and never for the mere purpose of curiosity.

I opened the square door at the back of the shop which faced the main entrance. As was usual on a hot day the door at the entrance was propped open by pieces of flannelette and towelling, and through this open portal there came to my ears a confused babel of sound. The shop was empty of customers, the assistants stood about in groups, and, what was most surprising of all, my father, who was usually at this hour bustling about in his shirt-sleeves, was standing in formal attire talking to a policeman.

I tiptoed up to him as quietly as I could; for some reason or other I felt that any unnecessary noise would be an indiscretion. The policeman went away and my father smiled and said: 'Let's have a look outside, shall we?'

The market square was full of people and the half-dozen policemen who constituted the town's police force had linked arms with a number of helpful citizens to hold back the crowd. In the space thus provided were a fire engine and two or three hand-pumps. The fire engine had a fat, round, stumpy boiler which looked something like a large milk churn painted red. The chief of the fire brigade was giving instructions to a man who was unharnessing the horses. The chief was wearing a uniform and a fire helmet which reminded me of pictures I had seen of Britannia. The other members of the fire brigade were hatless and in shirt-sleeves. The majority of them were working the hand-pumps. The men stood six aside, their hands on the long wooden handle of the pump, which was jerked up and down in a more or less rhythmic movement. Someone was giving them the time, crying: 'Up—down—up—down,' and I saw the white hands of the men rise and fall, rise and fall, and heard the pump go 'clank—clank—clank—clank.' It fascinated me to see the row of hands moving up and down. It seemed as though the wooden rail was lifting and lowering the hands of the men rather than being propelled by them; as though the men's arms were attached to some horrible instrument from which they were unable to free themselves, the tyrannical energy of which compelled them to contort their bodies in a constant movement of bending and stretching.

The remaining members of the fire brigade were directing the water from the nozzles of the hoses in an endeavour to quench the flames. There were no fire ladders and these men stood in the street or were perched on the roofs of the adjoining houses.

The fire was gaining in strength and now began to roar with savage triumph. The air was thick with sparks, and black smuts fell like a dark snow over the uneasy heads of the crowd below the police cordon.

The policeman who had spoken to my father reappeared and said something in a low voice. My father said 'Now?' and the policeman nodded his head. My father spoke to the assistants and then took me by the arm and led me indoors, where he told my mother that every one must leave the house as the fire was spreading and moving in our direction.

We began to get our things together and presently the assistants came down the stairs carrying coats and suitcases, and headed by my father, who was wrapped in an enormous ulster, we trooped out of the house. My mother held my hand and we followed the bulky, overclad figure of my father up the narrow lane at the side of the garden. Behind us the assistants, clad in a variety of hastily donned garments, scrambled over the loose stones of the lane while cook, stout and panting, brought up the rear.

At the top of the hill we turned into a meadow and leaned over a wooden fence to watch the flames below. Up here the air was clear and gay; below a pall of smoke hung over the town. My father had recently given me an illustrated copy of Bunyan's *Pilgrim's Progress*. It was a stock line from the shop, but though reduced from 2s. 6d. to 9¾d. it would not sell. Now as I looked at the canopy of smoke above the houses below I felt like Christian fleeing from the City of Destruction.

The 'young ladies' were bubbling over with excitement and Mr. Tomkins was holding forth like a guide showing a party of sightseers a spectacle of peculiar interest. I kept running from one to the other, anxious to hear all that was being said. My mother stood by my father, who encouraged her with cheerful and optimistic remarks.

The fire had started about eleven o'clock in the morning and it was now afternoon. We grew hungry and my mother handed round biscuits and chocolate. Then we grew thirsty, but there was nothing to drink. Another two hours went by and the smoke below had almost disappeared. We could see the factory like a black patch among the red and brown houses of the town. Over this black patch was a thin eddy of drifting smoke. My father was of the opinion that we might now return and this suggestion was received with acclamation.

Back at Cornhill House we found the building untouched except for a certain amount of dirt on stairs and passages where firemen had ascended to the roof. The fire had been put out, but little was left of the factory except the walls.

Cook and my mother got together a fine spread—a sort of extra high high tea. Every one set to with a will, but although I enjoyed an egg and my favourite blackberry jam, I felt tired and irritable. Even this wonderful meal seemed something of an anticlimax after the day's events.

CHAPTER XI

DREAMS AND A FOREST

In the summer following the factory fire I had a succession of nightmares. One dream above all others occurred constantly. I was walking along a flat, empty countryside. The ground was pitted with craters between which were stacks of ochrous rock. I walked without any sensation of movement or feeling of progression. The place reminded me of pictures I had seen of the surface of the moon; the predominant colour was lunar, and a thin yellow light fell from an invisible sky. I do not know exactly what it was about this dream that frightened me; I think it was the sense of desolation and the intense stillness as of death.

I went in such fear of these dreams that I dreaded the coming of night and was reluctant to go to bed. Each evening I begged that I might remain up a little longer, using any and every excuse to effect delay, but concealing my real reason in obstinate pride. The dreams continued and I began to walk in my sleep, possibly as a subconscious effort to escape from my dream. Once I came downstairs and entered the lighted room in which my mother and father were sitting. My father said: 'Go back to your room,' and still asleep I returned to bed.

On another occasion I awoke in the middle of the night to find myself in such utter darkness that it seemed to fill my mouth like a dark puff-ball. Something hard was pressed against my back and when I put out my hand it came into contact with a number of vertical bars. I shouted in terror and my father came out of his bedroom carrying a candle, to find me sitting halfway down the stairs.

A doctor was called in to examine me and stated that I was suffering from a nervous disorder. It was necessary, he said, that I should go away to a quiet place where I should have plenty of fresh air and be quite alone, or at least come into contact with very few people. This seemed an insoluble problem, for if I was to be alone who would look after me, and if I stayed with friends how was I to be alone? It was then that my mother remembered an acquaintance, an old lady called Maggie, who lived by herself in the depths of the New Forest, and it was finally decided that I should go there to stay for a week or so.

I remember very little about Maggie except that she was bright of face and eye, kindly disposed, and did everything to make me comfortable. But I have a very clear picture of the cottage, which was small and putty-coloured and might have served for a stage setting or for the barley-sugar cottage of fairy lore. It stood not among trees, but in a wide clearing. Behind it the ground sloped upwards to the edge of the forest and the brown thatch of the cottage roof fell against the rising ground like matted hair thrown back from a sallow face. I remember, too, Maggie's cat called Jes, short for Jeshurun who, according to Deuteronomy, 'waxed fat and kicked.' Jes took a fancy to me and during supper sat on a nearby shelf level with my head and watched me eat. And in the morning when I woke up in the attic, which smelt of apples and lavender, Jes was sitting at the foot of my bed solemnly regarding me as though I was a curiosity to him, which no doubt I was.

But what I remember most about that time is the forest itself; the majesty and dignity of the trees, and the feeling they gave me as they stood rank on rank, of withheld power.

I spent the greater part of my days in the forest, and almost at once my dreams and nightmares left me and did not return. I set off each morning with a satchel of sandwiches and cake and a medicine bottle of cold tea, and wandered and rested at will until early evening. I saw no one, but I was not lonely. The wooded glades were warm, and pine-needles made a soft springy carpet for my feet. A thousand tiny sounds kept me company; the voices of innumerable insects chirruped to the chorus of bird-song; boughs and branches of trees creaked and rasped while their leaves rustled and twittered continually. The whole forest muttered, talked, sang, and laughed under the sun. I felt at one with it, a part of it; it was only at twilight that I was a stranger there. Then silence fell, birds and insects were quiet, the leaves of the trees still. I felt a little frightened. It was like the sudden silence at a party when someone has said the wrong thing. I felt guilty as though it was I who was responsible for this hushed, embarrassing silence. I walked softly, quickly, glad to leave the forest behind me. I ran down the slope to Maggie's cottage, very conscious of the semicircle of darkening trees standing motionless behind me.

During my stay in the forest I learnt to climb trees. I had long desired to do this, but in the company of others was too self-conscious and fearful of failure to make the attempt. Now that I was alone, and with an endless number of trees from which to choose, I set about the task with confidence and resolution. I made careful mental note of the position of the branches and their shape and size and distance from one another. Then I began to climb, keeping close to the trunks of the trees, but moving round if I found a bough conveniently situated and within easy reach.

In this way I gained the top and felt the strong moving air about my face and head. Above, at great distance, fleecy clouds moved in irregular formation across the uncharted sky; below the swaying tree-tops engulfed me in a sea of leaves which, as the wind swung over them, leapt towards me like a wave.

For a long time I rested on my lofty perch. The branches were so entangled that I was able to lean back upon them; my body accepted their motion; I floated like a swimmer at rest, rising and falling with a gentle undulation. Between the interlacing foliage sunlight flashed and twinkled like darting brilliant-hued fish, and small currents of air, lost in the intricate maze, touched my limbs in passing as though with timid gestures they sought assurance in their endless quest.

My senses were heightened and empowered to receive countless impressions. I felt an enchantment that I could not formulate in words, an ecstasy which in later years, when custom and experience had made the mind less receptive, I could never quite recover.

CHAPTER XII

MY FATHER'S BUSINESS

In the meantime, while I was coming to my first fumbling conclusions with life, my father worked long hours to establish his business. He did a strictly cash trade, unusual in those days of 'family' business when to 'open an account' with a tradesman was to confer a privilege, in return for which the customer expected obsequious attention and long credit. My father's customers were drawn from the working people and the families of agricultural labourers. The basis of his business was 'small profits, quick returns.' Those were the days of free trade when competition was fierce and unrestricted and profits 'cut to the bone.' Slogans such as 'Get On or Get Out,' 'The Nimble Penny,' 'Take Care of the Pence and the Pound will take care of Itself,' were universally accepted as unquestionable truths, as indeed they were. It was a ruthless and relentless age which demanded of the moderately successful hard work, temperate habits, prudence, thrift, and all the other inglorious and unglamorous virtues of Smilesian self-help.

To celebrate the first year of trading my father held an anniversary sale. I give below extracts from the circular, a four-page sheet containing about one hundred and forty items, which he caused to be distributed in thousands throughout the neighbouring towns and villages. It requires little comment. The phraseology gives some idea of my father's vigour and directness of approach and also his sense of showmanship. The prices speak for themselves. In the modern American idiom they might be said to reach 'a new low.' Indeed, I doubt whether such prices have existed before or since. Two facts at least can be deduced — the low standard of living of the common people and the narrow trading margin of the shopkeeper. I might also add a third—namely, the shrewd buying and business acumen displayed by my father.

Here is the circular in a much reduced form:

HANCOCK'S ANNIVERSARY SALE

WE INTEND TO SIGNALIZE the approach of our first anniversary in the town by giving away a good amount of the Profit on our Goods, and off some other Stocks we have bought quite lately. Relying not upon what we have done, but rather upon what we propose doing, we are sure you will appreciate the SALE we are preparing for your excitement and profit.

We have been agreeably impressed by the friendliness and good judgment displayed by the local people. *They know a cheap line when they see it!* We have made a fair start in our first year, but we want to do better in the second. No pains will be spared to achieve that object. Courtesy, promptness, and absolute honesty with every customer, combined with real good value for cash and cash only. These methods we consider will end in re‐establishing this old‐world draper's shop on a new and surer foundation.

ESTABLISHED OVER A CENTURY as a Linen Draper's,

it will now, we trust, rise again like a phoenix from the ashes of its own dead past.

READ DOWN THESE COLUMNS

Dress materials
3 good colours
Double width
$2\frac{3}{4}d.$ per yard.

CORSETS
at $6\frac{3}{4}d.$ & $11\frac{1}{4}d.$
per pair

Long waisted
Double Busk
Corsets, black
Satin Cloth
$1/0\frac{3}{4}d.$ per pair
Equal in appearance to $1/11\frac{3}{4}d.$

Prints $1\frac{3}{4}d.$ & $2\frac{3}{4}d.$

Frillings $1d.$ &
$1\frac{1}{4}d.$

40-in. Apron Cloth:
$2\frac{3}{4}d.$

Black and Navy
Serges $6\frac{3}{4}d.$ to $2/3\frac{3}{4}d.$

Ladies' & children's
Baskets of Gloves
$1\frac{3}{4}d.$, $2\frac{3}{4}d.$, and $4\frac{3}{4}d.$

72-in. white Twill
sheeting $6\frac{3}{4}d.$ yd.

£80 worth of calico
from $2d.$ per yard.

Tie-Ups $1\frac{3}{4}d.$ Baby's
opportunity

Following lines of
Fancy Goods will be
swept out: 70 Pictures 11 in. by 15 in.
$6\frac{3}{4}d.$ Postcard Albums
$1\frac{3}{4}d.$ Pearl Necklaces $2\frac{3}{4}d.$ Oak
Frames to hold 3
photos $2\frac{3}{4}d.$

Thick Flannelette
Petticoats $11\frac{3}{4}d.$

Towels $1d.$, $1\frac{3}{4}d.$, and
$3\frac{3}{4}d.$

Children's Cashmere
socks all sizes
Black, Navy and Tan
$2\frac{3}{4}d.$ per pair. (Don't
Darn!!!)

Hemstitched Handkerchiefs $1d.$ each.
Hold these up to the
light, they'll bear
it!!

JACKETS, HATS, and FLOWERS are to be marked so that they will go like magic!

All ends and bits of FLANNEL, CALICO, DRESSES, LININGS, and other Material are being measured. If you want to see them, hold them or they will vanish before your very eyes!

MEN'S CLOTHING DEPARTMENT

There are a Big lot of Black suits, Trousers and coats. Good quality stuff, but their Days at Hancock's are numbered!	MEN'S Collars 1d. and 2¾d.	SOLDIERS' OVERCOATS Have to go 'quick March.' 2/11½ and 4/11½
	CYCLE SUITS Lined flannel 4/11½	
		50 MEN'S HATS 1/- Worth 3/6
200 PAIRS of MEN'S Trousers 1/- to 3/11½ Pair. Every Man in his right mind will be clothed!	Tweed Cycle Knickers 1/11½ Worth three times the money.	MEN'S TIES 1d. and 1¾d.
	4 MEN'S 25/- Black suits at 9/11½ per suit.	MEN'S AND BOYS' CAPS 2¾d. to 11½d.

DON'T forget the doors are not open till 12 o'clock on Thursday.

DON'T grumble if you are locked out—we can only let in so many at one time.

DON'T come without your purse or you will see other people get the plums.

DON'T wait till Saturday night before you come to have a look.

These low prices, as the introduction to the circular makes clear, were partially the result of the purchase of a bankrupt stock at a considerable discount. At first sight this looks like an easy way of making money out of the misfortunes of others. In actual fact it was not so simple. There was usually a great deal of competition for these stocks and the prospective purchaser had often to travel some distance to view them. The stock was in most cases on view at the shop of the unfortunate bankrupt and was there displayed to best

*C

advantage and in the most tempting manner. The retailer who came to view was looking for something that approximated to his own class of trade; also like every other kind of buyer he was looking for something good or something scarce which could be bought at the lowest price. The brightest and cleanest part of the stock, and the goods most in demand, were therefore given the foremost place on the tables and counters, and moreover dressed out with all the arts and graces at the command of window-dresser and display expert. Like the customer he serves, the draper is consciously or unconsciously intimidated by the art of display— the cunning blending of texture, line, and colour has its effect upon the most hardened mind. But the experienced buyer knows that he must look also behind the counter, under the tables, and in the darkest fixtures at the back of the shop, where perhaps the bulk of the stock he thinks of buying is to be found. And he may then discover dress materials of a loud and unpleasing pattern, coats and dresses of unfashionable cut and design, trimmings, edgings, and beadings long out of date.

When my father bought a stock we were always curious to look at the queer oddments which came with it. One such stock contained, in addition to the more saleable items, hundreds of lapel buttons containing a portrait of General Buller of Boer War fame; two bundles of assorted walking-sticks with dogs' heads; a quantity of men's black suits (the original owner probably did a large mourning order trade), a collection of colonial flags; and about five hundred yards of yosemites or brilliants—a kind of dimity used for children's dresses.

The particular stock mentioned in the sale catalogue came from the Isle of Wight. My father took train to Southampton and hired for five pounds a pantechnicon which he arranged to take with him on the boat to the island. This, of course, was a risk, since he was not sure whether he was going to need it. The journey was made during a snowstorm and my father was almost the only passenger on board. He therefore came to the conclusion that in this instance there would be very little competition, and made a tender for the stock at the exceptional discount of 66½ per cent. The gamble came off, but his difficulties were not yet over. Once the stock was his, it became his responsibility to remove it. He obtained the assistance of a man who had formerly been employed in the shop that was now closed and together they removed the goods from the shop into the pantechnicon.

The stock was listed in pencil in a dilapidated sort of washing-book and many of the items were almost indecipherable. At last, as they were ready to move off, my father said:

'Well, is that the lot?'

'Yes, sir,' was the reply, 'it 's all accounted for.'

My father, however, decided to have one last look round and in doing so discovered under a dark counter a quantity of goods, including the 'brilliants' already mentioned.

They had been working against time and as a result of this delay my father nearly lost the boat. The pantechnicon was run aboard and hastily secured. The weather had still further deteriorated, it was snowing harder than ever, and a high wind was blowing. The journey had barely commenced when the pantechnicon broke loose and charged across the narrow deck of the small steamer. Fortunately it did not go overboard, but the sudden transference of weight gave the boat a decided list.

In spite of these vicissitudes the stock was eventually brought home, and now began the task of sorting, listing, and pricing for the sale. When the unsale-able items had been accounted for, and the remains of the stock priced, the average profit was little more than normal. But my father enjoyed his adventure and the low prices were certainly an advertisement which did much to establish the business. So many things were sold at $2\frac{3}{4}d.$ that it became locally a sort of catchword. Sometimes when I went for a walk with my parents small boys would run up behind us and shout: 'Hancock's two free—all you want for two free fardings.'

Quite apart from the reduced costs offered by the purchase of a bankrupt stock, prices in those days were generally very low. There were four main reasons for this, namely keen competition, the poverty of the working people, the cheapness of foodstuffs coupled with a low standard of living, and the fact that the retailer himself lived very much more economically than he does to-day.

Every draper had his own special 'low price line,' which served to establish him in the public mind for that particular article. Household linens, especially calicoes, and what were known as 'bread and cheese' lines were 'cut' in prices. Thirty-six-inch-wide calico was bought at $2\frac{1}{2}d.$ per yard, or even at $2\frac{5}{8}d.$ per yard, and sold at $2\frac{3}{4}d.$ per yard.

It must be remembered that white and unbleached calico was used in those days for nearly every article of women's underclothing. The modern silk step-ins and panties, or even the cheaper artificial silk and stockinette underwear of to-day, were unknown—at least among the great mass of the female population. The time had not yet arrived when Miss O'Grady could dress like the colonel's lady. Dress was still an 'outward and visible sign' of class distinction. So calico was a basic need, a sort of common denominator, the value and price of which decided the draper's position and fixed his status in the public mind.

In the larger towns, where women demanded a more showy or fashionable dress, this cutting of prices extended to materials such as chiffons and muslins. To the retailer this was a serious problem, since this type of article—easily shop-soiled and in colours which quickly went out of fashion—was expected to bear a high rate of profit.

Before setting up in business for himself, my father was employed in a London suburban shop. On the opposite side of the street was a larger and more ambitious store. One day the larger shop displayed a whole window of fashionable dress muslins at $6\frac{3}{4}d.$ per yard. My father's employer was unable to buy in such quantity or sell at such a low figure, so he did the next best thing. He sent an apprentice across the road to purchase two dozen yards of his competitor's muslins at the retail price. He cut off three yards and put the rest in his fixture. The three yards were tastefully arranged round a fat cardboard block and displayed in the window at the same price as his rival. This brought him no profit and naturally no one who saw the magnificent display opposite was going to purchase the muslin from the shop which modestly exhibited one single piece. But what this manœuvre did accomplish, and at very little cost, was to rob the big shop of the value of exclusiveness. People said: 'Oh, yes, So-and-so has a wonderful display of muslins, but I see that Jones, opposite, has got it too and at the same price.'

CHAPTER XIII

CIRCULARS AND CUSTOMERS

To distribute the sale circulars round the countryside my father employed a Mr. Cole, who made a somewhat precarious living by performing such odd jobs. He was assisted by his son, a cheerful, flaxen-haired youth of eighteen, who because of his father's failing sight, drove the wagonette which conveyed them to the villages and towns round about. The wagonette was old, and creaked and groaned to every movement of its wheels. Here and there, scattered about its body like a rash, were patches of sun-blistered paint. These patches represented the older parts of the vehicle; new spokes to the wheels and pieces of wood more recently added to its sides remained unpainted. The horse between the shafts was also old and matched the wagonette itself, even to the point of being covered with spots of dullish brown colour, as though it too had once known a complete coat of paint.

While the Coles were busily engaged in fetching and carrying the sale circulars from the shop, it was my delight to mount the small steps at the rear of the wagonette and to climb up on the elevated front seat, from which vantage point I felt very important. It gave me a particular interest to pull over the lever which applied the brake, and it would sometimes happen that when the Coles finally started off, with a great deal of clicking of the tongue and guttural objurgations to the faithful and patient horse, I would remember that I had left the brake on. As, however, the rubber of the brake had long since become worn to the thinness of a crescent moon, and had little or no effect upon the speed of the wheels, this oversight on my part did not greatly matter.

The sale became a biannual event and sometimes in the summer my parents would accompany the Coles on their journey and take me with them to help with the distribution of the sale circulars. We made a round trip of about twenty miles and each village or town within that area was circularized thoroughly. On our arrival at a village the horse and wagonette were left in an inn yard and my father drew up a plan of campaign. Each of us was assigned to a street or row of cottages and then we set off, carrying the circulars in satchels.

I enjoyed delivering the circulars partly because I felt I was doing a real job of work, but chiefly, I think, because of the interest I found in the different types of houses and gardens. I had to learn the technique (if such a word can be employed for a task which at first sight would seem to need only unskilled labour) necessary to ensure that the sale bill actually got into the house—and what was more important, into the house of a potential customer.

Every garden gate had its own peculiarity. Some opened to the lift of a latch, others required the sliding of a bolt or the lifting of a ring, and some refused to open at all or gave at last to a combination of various stratagems, and then only when performance in the right order of sequence was attained.

Wooden gates jammed, iron gates dragged or needed lifting—each and every one had its own eccentricity and answered the more readily to sym-pathetic humouring, without which they groaned or squeaked, whined, and complained in their different fashions. There was the light, tricky gate which answered readily to the deft touch but resisted un-skilled force, and the heavy comatose gate which hung weightily upon its hinges like a sluggard to his bed and responded only to bludgeoning, brutal strength.

Having negotiated the gate, the next problem was the front door. Some had knockers protruding like a heavy nose over the blackened mouth of the letter-box. Residential houses of the 'villa' type had a brass letter-box, the flap of which was so powerful that it would catch the fingers when the sale circular was slipped through.

But most of the cottages had neither knocker nor letter-box and the circular had to be pushed under the door. Here another problem presented itself. The bottom of many of the front doors was covered with a wooden slat to keep out driving rain, and in this case the only method of introducing the circular was to rap on the door and wait for someone to open it; and then trust to luck, the power of personal persuasion, and the good humour of the occupier.

Occasionally a whiskered, irate labourer would fling open the door and demand: 'Who asked thee to come a-trapesing and a-knocking? Get thee off down along the way thee come.' But such occasions were rare. The majority of the country folk welcomed the circulars. Few of them ever saw a newspaper except perhaps on Sundays; there were no books in the house and the sale bill was an unexpected gift of reading matter which they read slowly and laboriously from cover to cover. Sometimes we ran across an old customer, who would insist upon us having tea with her, and we were given strong tea off the hob and bread and butter and cake which was eaten in the old Somerset fashion—a bite of bread and butter and then a bite of cake—finishing them together instead of reserving the cake to the last.

Tuesday was market day, when the farmers came to town. Occasionally they were accompanied by their wives, who because of their rare visits found a great deal of shopping to do. Some of them were in our shop for the greater part of the day selecting household goods, dress materials, and underclothing for themselves, and caps, ties, and socks and suits for their husbands and sons, and even for the husbands and sons of their neighbours.

On those days my father provided refreshments—a glass of sherry and a biscuit at eleven o'clock, and for the more important customers a sit-down midday meal of roast beef, vegetables, Yorkshire pudding, and apple tart.

The meal was served on a trestle table, which was set up in what was known as the Manchester room— a semi-basement at the rear of the shop. In this room with its low ceiling and stone - flagged floor were kept the reserve blankets, flannelettes, also rolls of oilcloth and linoleum. It was also used for unpacking crates, boxes, and bales of new goods, brought in from the side street through double doors which opened on to a flight of stone steps.

On market day all of us, including the assistants, had dinner with the customers. It was no unusual thing for twenty people to sit round the table, where the farmers, after a morning in the cattle market, could join their wives.

When I returned home from school on market day I would sometimes forget this arrangement and walk into the dining-room only to find the table unlaid, the chairs pushed under the table; the room conveyed a sense of unusual emptiness because I had expected the bustling activity that accompanies the preparation of a meal.

Then my mother, who had heard me come in—or perhaps remembered my absent-mindedness—would come out of the kitchen in search of me, her face flushed, features tightened to an unusual degree by the stress and strain of the morning's work, so that her face assumed an unnatural aspect at once hard and fragile; and the general tension of her manner would confuse and embarrass me without my being aware of the cause of my embarrassment.

'Hurry up,' she would say. 'Dinner is in the Manchester room. Run upstairs and wash your face and hands. There is water in my room and you can use my face flannel.'

In my parents' bedroom I hung about and dawdled over my washing for no recognizable reason, for I was uneasy in this room. I felt that I was intruding, invading a privacy that should remain inviolate. It was not a familiar room and it was seldom that I saw my parents in it; to be in it alone gave me a feeling of trespassing.

Yet there was nothing unusual about the room, it was not depressing. The sun shone through the window and the brass knobs on the bedstead sparkled in the sunlight. The pictures were ordinary and homely. There was a picture of a Scottish lady saying to a gentleman in kilts: 'And will you no come back again?' And there was a picture of an angel with a gentle face and outspread wings; and just over the wash-hand stand hung a framed photograph of the very ordinary house in Chiswick in which I had been born.

My day-dreaming was interrupted by my mother's voice calling me and the clang of the dinner bell. I tipped some water from the ewer and dabbed my face with my mother's face flannel—a sort of knitted glove which had the smell of stale cold-cream soap. Then I ran downstairs, through the shop door, and into the Manchester room.

Every one was seated except my mother, who stood with her back to me, carving the joint. The people sat in line on each side of the narrow table; behind them were rolls of linoleum so tall that they extended to the ceiling and gave the impression of supporting it like pillars in a church. A shaft of sunlight from a tiny window in a corner of the further wall fell diagonally across the table, illuminated the faces of the seated people, and brought into prominence a patch of red oilcloth. It made me think of pictures I had seen in the Bible—light falling on the face of the infant Samuel, or on holy men, or divines, except that the faces here looked more homely than holy. The ray of light and the dim background further enhanced the illusion that I was looking at an early steel engraving in which the artist had emphasized the central figures against a background of an indeterminate character.

I found myself seated next to a jolly, red-faced farmer, who tipped me sixpence. This was an unusual event, and I immediately felt very kindly disposed to this particular farmer, who must surely be a paragon among his kind. I did not know that he had just effected a most lucrative deal in the cattle market, and moreover had persuaded my father to knock two shillings off his wife's bill.

CHAPTER XIV

THE SHOP

As I grew older I was allowed to help in the shop, especially at sale time, stock-taking, and during the Christmas rush. One of the features of the summer sale was the introduction of two - shilling bundles. These bundles were brown-paper parcels containing pieces of lace, remnants of dress material, towelling, odd sizes in gloves, stockings, and corsets, and many other articles that had been left over during the year's trading. A sample bundle might contain a blouse, a pair of corsets, a remnant of print, a packet of needles, and a reel of cotton. These assorted articles bought separately would cost two or three times the price of the bundle, but in order to effect a clearance and as an advertisement they were offered collectively and anonymously for two shillings.

The customer did not know what she was going to get for her money; it was a 'pig in a poke,' but she knew from hearsay or experience that it would be reasonably 'good pig.' Incidentally the phrase 'a pig in a poke' as applied in this instance is appropriate, for goods 'jobbed out' or returned to the wholesaler as unsuitable were referred to in the trade as 'cold pig.'

The two-shilling bundles were placed in a large tub, the exterior of which was swathed in decorative coloured paper. It was my job to stand by the tub as custodian and salesman. The potential customer would dip her hand into the remotest corners of the tub in the belief that the best is always furthest away, and feel the bundles at the bottom, or even lift them out and examine their shape and contours in the hope of guessing the nature of their contents. She knew her choice was a gamble, but she wished to reduce the element of chance to a minimum. Having made her choice she paid me and I took the money to the cash-desk and returned with a bill as receipt.

It was a simple job and when business was quiet I had time to look about me. The shop was rectangular in shape with ample floor space and a lofty ceiling. Behind me were the windows and in front the main counter which contained an opening in the middle, through which one passed to gain access to the Manchester room, or to ascend a flight of stairs to the show-room. On my left were the 'office' and cash-desk, mounted on a raised platform and partitioned off from the rest of the shop by wooden panels surrounded by glazed glass. Originally the interior of the office had been comparatively roomy, but as the years went by an accumulation of trade catalogues, ledgers, stock-books, old invoices, and the like piled in apparent disorder on projecting shelves had reduced the office to a species of cubby-hole, so that a certain dexterity was required of any one who ventured in or out. Moreover, the office was the repository for stocks of business stationery, such as letter heads, counter check-books, price tickets, and window-bills. In addition it had become a lumber-room for articles of a miscellaneous character. Every sort of oddity seemed to find its way there—a dolls' house, a glue-pot, a tattered dictionary, a broken chisel. The word odd was prominently displayed on cardboard boxes labelled 'odd string,' 'odd screws,' and 'odd gum-paper,' for everything, no matter how small, was saved and sorted. The first duty of an apprentice in those days was to pick up pins and lengths of string from the shop floor. There was also in a railed-off corner of the office a collection of articles left behind and unclaimed by customers, which included a broken umbrella, a child's game of ludo, a cake of carbolic soap, and, oddest of all, a billiard cue.

In front of the cash till, nailed to a wooden rail in awful warning, were counterfeit coins—a bad penny, a cracked half-crown, and a lead florin.

The cash till itself was simple and uncomplicated; it consisted of a single drawer divided into sections, each containing a shallow wooden bowl for the accommodation of every kind of coin from the aristocratic sovereign to the humble farthing.

I have described the farthing as a humble coin, but it played a large part. Nearly all the prices of goods in the shop had three-farthings tacked on to the end of them. It was a trade convention, introduced to give an illusion of cheapness. A table-cloth marked one and eleven three-farthings looked considerably less costly than one marked two shillings. The solid uncompromising figure had an air of stern and terrible finality.

Thus the farthing change became a dominating feature in all change. But the number of these small coins was limited and the majority of people objected to them as inconvenient and comparatively useless. This in turn gave rise to the custom of giving a small article as a farthing change.

The customer had a wide choice and was able to select her farthing change from a varied assortment of articles which included pens, pencils, packets of needles, cases of thread, hairpins, hat-pins, press studs, and collar studs.

One of the favourite farthing changes was a folding card containing six assorted sewing needles. The outside covers of the card were printed in colour and contained a portrait of Shakespeare's house, Anne Hathaway's cottage, and Stratford-on-Avon church.

What connection there could be between Shakespeare and needles, I have not the slightest idea.

I was glad that my tub of two-shilling bundles stood near the open doorway, for the day was hot.

Outside the sun drenched the market square in quivering heat. In the sharp clear light the houses seemed to lean backwards as if to take shelter within their own shade. The town hall appeared to be un-affected by the sun; it stood solid and majestic, deter-mined to maintain its municipal dignity. A dog, its tongue lolling out, moved slowly across the deserted square and flopped down in an angle of shade cast by the town hall steps. The slate roofs of the houses opposite gleamed like burnished steel. A group of pigeons stepped daintily over the roof-tops and made fluttering ascents into the air, as though to escape the heat of the sun-baked tiles.

The warmth of the day accentuated the characteristic smells of the interior of the shop. There was the hot muffled dampish smell of blankets and flannels, the rank farmyard smell of corduroys, and from the open doorway, mingled with the odour of dust from the street, came the smell of dyes from the cretonnes and chintzes 'dressed out' round the windows and entrance lobbies. The feeling of warmth was in no way diminished by the sight of my father buying woollens and fleecy underclothing from a traveller. Winter goods were invariably bought in advance during the summer months, so as to enable the wholesaler and manufacturers to obtain some idea of the quantity required to be made; and as an inducement to the retailer to place a forward order he was granted special terms.

Even now, during the month of August, winter goods were already arriving, and at the counter opposite

the cash desk I could see the assistants sewing small
tickets on the new goods—a process known as 'tab-
bing.' The word tab had also another meaning—
it was applied by the assistants to a customer who
when presented with an assortment of goods was
unable to make up her mind as to her choice, admired
at length first the one and then the other and ended
up by buying nothing at all. I do not know the
origin of this word. The word tabby is a general
term for waved or watered silk or shot silks which
change their shade in different lights. Perhaps the
expression 'to tab' derives from this idea of something
changeable.

The somewhat lethargic preoccupations of the shop
on this summer afternoon were interrupted by spas-
modic bursts of activity when customers made their
appearance. At one moment the shop would be
empty and at the next three or four customers would
enter together. At once, like a machine set in motion,
the various component parts of the business went into
action. Customers moved from one counter to another, made inquiries, fingered materials, seated themselves on chairs, and pulled out shopping lists or
patterns to be matched. Assistants bustled about,
took down boxes, opened packets and cases, and made
polite conversation while they displayed their goods
in the most seductive manner they could devise.
Above the murmur of conversation there rose two
distinct sounds, the ringing of electric bells and the
rumbling, bumbling note of the cash railway. The
bells were used to summon assistants from one part
of the shop to another. If they were short-handed in
the show-room they rang for someone to come up,
and alternatively if the shop downstairs was crowded a
button was pressed to obtain assistance from the

show-room. Sometimes the bell downstairs would give two short rings, which indicated that the assistant in the show-room was in difficulties with a customer, who was perhaps on the point of leaving without making a purchase, thus necessitating my father's presence to give added persuasion or advice, and so prevent a 'swop' or loss of sale.

Originally the phrase 'to get the swop' was a slang expression meaning to be dismissed from employment. At one time firms kept a record of the number of customers that an assistant allowed to leave without making a purchase. If these occasions exceeded a certain number the assistant was discharged as incompetent. This system, which tyrannized both buyer and seller alike, since the one thought in the mind of the assistant was to effect a sale at whatever cost, even if the thing sold was totally unsuitable to the customer, was already in decline. And thus the word 'swop,' though still distantly associated with the fear of dismissal, had now come to mean merely the loss of a sale.

I have mentioned another sound heard in the shop when business was brisk—a deeper sound, a dull reverberation, a bass note to the shrill treble of the electric bells. This was produced by the rolling balls of the cash railway.

Our system had been in use for some time. It consisted of an overhead railway suspended from the ceiling along which wooden balls almost the size of croquet balls trundled along to the cash-desk. There were several routes, but the main line was the one from the men's outfitting department, situated on the other side of a private passage that gave access to the domestic side of the house.

When Mr. Tomkins of the 'outfits' served a customer and required change, he unscrewed the wooden ball of the cash railway and put money and duplicate bill inside.   Then, screwing the two halves of the ball together, he placed it in a small lift which was drawn up to the railway by a cord.   When the lift reached the top, one of its sides fell open and the ball was tilted down a steep incline to give it the necessary momentum to roll along the line until it reached the cash-desk.   Here it fell down a shoot and landed on a bell-push, which rang a buzzer to announce its arrival.   Whereupon the cashier took out the money, filed the duplicate, put back the change, and the whole process was repeated in reverse.

CHAPTER XV

HOLIDAYS AND APARTMENTS

I spent my first holiday at the seaside with my parents when I was ten years old. On the eve of our departure rain fell steadily and I went to bed in a gloomy and despondent frame of mind. The next morning I woke early to find the sun streaming into my room, but when I jumped out of bed and ran to the window I saw that the pavements were wet and there was a watery gleam in the eye of the sun.

Breakfast was a makeshift affair. My mother was hollow-eyed and tired; she had been up half the night packing an enormous trunk. The time for our departure seemed to crawl, but eventually the station bus arrived and the trunk was hoisted on to the roof and secured with straps. Even then there were other bags and packages to be carried, including my father's Gladstone bag and a long wicker basket with hold-all attachment through which were thrust umbrellas and my mother's best cream sunshade.

The bus trundled us off to the station, the train arrived, and my father got a porter to put the big trunk in the guard's van.

When we reached our destination we left our luggage in the cloak-room and set out to find apartments. My parents had not booked accommodation; they preferred to look round for rooms on the spot. Looking back it seems strange that it should be possible to do this in the middle of the holiday season, but at that time the annual fortnight's holiday had not become a general habit and there was little possibility of our being squeezed out. On the contrary, landladies competed strenuously for our patronage.

We walked up the short street which led to the front and arrived at the clock tower. The sun, which had hitherto remained hidden by clouds, now emerged and shone warmly upon the bay, so that the brown sands became golden and the houses of the wide Georgian crescent met us with smiling faces.

I wanted to join the people on the sands where children were running about with buckets and spades or digging energetically at the water's edge. But my mother was afraid I might get lost.

I had once been lost in a crowd on a day excursion. True it was only for a very short time, a few minutes at most, during which I had stopped to watch a dog fight while my parents hurried on ahead to catch a train.

The memory of this incident remained very definitely in their minds, my escapade had caused delay, we nearly missed the train; and subsequently I was to hear on more than one occasion the story told of how I had been lost, and with each telling the experience grew more terrifying until at last I too began to feel that I had missed calamity by a hair's breath.

'You shall sit on the sands all day to-morrow, if you wish,' said my mother, and with this promise we set out on our search for suitable accommodation.

If I had known then the miles I was to walk, the number of steps and stairs I was to climb, and the queer interior odours I was to smell, I think I might have put up greater opposition to the idea of accompanying my parents.

My mother had a keen eye for detail and quite remarkable powers of deduction. Sometimes when we were sitting on a public seat, or at a table outside a café, she would speculate upon the habits, occupations, and interests of someone near by.

'You see that young lady over there,' she might remark; 'she is dressed in the fashion, too smart to belong to this district. She keeps turning round, she is waiting for someone, it is not her husband, she has no wedding-ring, she has only just come out, her shoes are not dusty,' and so on. And quite often by some chance remark overheard or incident observed, she would be proved almost entirely correct in her deductions.

This habit of observation proved of great value in apartment hunting. Nevertheless it was quite easy to go wrong in estimating the amenities of a house by its exterior. A bright, clean dwelling might house an eccentric landlady, or a shabby front camouflage an agreeable interior.

We sauntered along, glancing at each house that displayed a card announcing 'Apartments' or 'Board Residence,' and sometimes stopped to look at an attractive house that had no card of any kind, for occasionally the occupants of such a house might be willing to take a few people though too proud or independent to advertise the fact.

At the first house we tried (its windows were free of any kind of notice) the door was opened by a maidservant. At sight of us her mouth fell open in a gawp of surprise.

'Do you let rooms?' asked my father.

'I doan't know.'

'Is your mistress in?'

'I doan't know.'

'Will you please find out,' said my father.

The maid turned and fled. We waited and gazed into the spotless hall, which was furnished with a hatstand, a carved oak chair, and a mahogany table upon which stood an ornate brass gong. The linoleum-covered floor gleamed with the reflected glory of some powerful polish.

After what seemed a considerable time, a lady appeared dressed in a black taffeta dress protected by small black alpaca apron. She looked at me and then at my mother and said: 'I do not take children.'

'My little boy would cause you no trouble,' said my mother.

'I do not take children,' replied the lady in black. We left.

The next place we tried seemed admirable in every respect, except that the room which was to be allotted to me was at the top of the house and had a window-sill only a few inches from the floor.

'Oh, look at that window,' exclaimed my mother, 'how dangerous!' However, my father made a note in his pocket-book of the address, against which he wrote: 'Dangerous window.'

Another house we visited had lofty, airy rooms and gave every appearance of perfection. The landlady was pleasant and kindly. She had been cooking and she showed my mother an excellent roast in the oven. As we were leaving a large bleary-eyed man came blundering down the passage leaving in his wake a strong odour of whisky. 'My husband,' said the landlady apologetically. When the front door was closed behind us my father took out his note-book and wrote: 'Husband drinks.'

We passed a boarding-house which had a very attractive bow-window to the dining-room. 'How nice to sit in there and look out on the sea,' said my mother. She ascended the front door steps and peeped into the room. The tables were laid for dinner. 'Look at those forks,' said my mother. We looked. The prongs of the forks were coated yellow with egg. 'Badly washed,' said my mother. Just at that moment a woman with her hair down rushed into the room through one door and out through another, closely followed by an unshaven man in shirt-sleeves who was swearing violently. We turned away. There was no need for my father to take out his note-book.

We walked on and on, the sun grew hotter and hotter, I made audible lamentations. The entries in my father's book increased in number. 'No late meals,' 'Invalid son a half-wit,' 'No bath-room,' 'Lavatory in garden,' 'Children of house recovering from whooping-cough,' 'Queer smells.' The pages of the note-book began to look like a scene from the Grand Guignol.

Finally we returned to the house with the dangerous window. 'Perhaps something could be done about that window,' said my mother. My father hopefully agreed. 'Or perhaps he could have another room,' said my mother. 'It really was rather a nice house,' she added.

'Well, we'll see,' said my father. He too seemed to be feeling the strain.

We came to the house and this time a cheerful man opened the door. 'Come in, come in,' he said, in lively tones. 'I'm the landlord. You were here before, I think. Didn't like that window upstairs. Bit dangerous, eh? Well, I've fixed that. Come up and see.'

We went up. The landlord had screwed some wooden bars across the window. 'Oh, that's splendid,' said my mother. 'That is kind of you.'

I looked through the bars at the sands and the sun. Suddenly everything seemed perfect.

'You will be wanting some tea,' said the landlord. 'It's all ready for you downstairs.'

I turned round expectantly. My mother and father were smiling. We went down to tea.

On a later occasion, when we spent a holiday at a more distant seaside town, my parents, contrary to their usual custom, booked rooms in advance. They had seen a notice in the paper which advertised accommodation that was only 'three minutes from the station and three minutes from the sea.'

At the end of our journey, as we stood on the station platform, my father was approached by a seedy-looking individual who said: 'Am I addressing Mr. Hancock?'

'You are,' replied my father.

'Well, I 've come to show you the way to the house,' said the man. With that we set off, the seedy-looking individual walking slightly ahead.

'How very kind of them to look after us like this,' whispered my mother.

'I wonder,' said my father, doubtfully.

We walked down a long hill between houses and then began to ascend another hill which appeared to lead into the country.

'Are we going the right way?' inquired my father, who by this time was looking, as my mother would phrase it, 'pretty straight.'

'Oh, yes, sir,' said the man, 'this is a short cut.'

The 'three minutes to the station' had already elapsed. We had been walking now for nearly a quarter of an hour, the houses had been left behind, and open fields extended on either hand. My parents exchanged glances. Where was the man leading us? Was something wrong?

'Look here,' said my father at last, 'where ever are you taking us? Where is the house?'

'Almost there now, sir,' said the man. 'Look, over there.' And, sure enough, we could see in the distance a house standing by itself in the middle of a field.

At the door a slatternly-looking woman invited us in

to a small front room. 'This is the sitting-room,' she said; 'very comfortable, as you can see.'

We looked round and saw very little. The room was sparsely furnished with a table, two chairs, and what appeared to be a sofa.

'Ah, an ottoman,' said my father, sinking down wearily on the sofa. The next instant there was a hollow thud and my father sprang to his feet. The 'ottoman' was an empty deal box which had been covered with cotton chintz.

For a moment every one in the shabby room stood motionless like figures in a cheap tableau. Then my father said: 'We shall not be staying here. This is not what we were led to expect.' Nothing more was said and we walked out.

'But where is the sea?' I asked.

'Of course,' said my father, 'three minutes to the sea.' We looked round and presently caught sight of the sea beyond a row of trees. 'It certainly looks near,' said my father. 'Just out of curiosity we will judge for ourselves.'

We walked in the direction of the water at a normal pace. My father held his repeater watch in his hand. In three minutes exactly we came to the edge of a precipitous cliff; the sea was below, but there was no way down.

D

CHAPTER XVI

I VISIT UNCLE THEODORE

I SAT in a corner seat opposite my mother and watched her head nodding in sleep. The train gathered speed, the humming wheels beat out a steady rhythmic sound.

We were on our way to visit my mother's brother in Kent. By nightfall I should see for the first time my Uncle Theodore, my Aunt Ada, and my two cousins. Aunt Martha would be there also to welcome and make a fuss of me.

We had the compartment to ourselves. I got up and inspected the pictures above the seat. There was a photo of Bournemouth front and another of the 'Globe' at Swanage. In the middle was a large map with thick red veins running out of London, the heart, into the long limb of south-west England, and into the shorter podgy bit that was Kent. I was able to trace with my finger the route we were taking. When I had done this I sat down again and looked out of the window. I saw a flock of birds resting on the telegraph wires. The little fat blobs on the wires made a musical score for the stately dance of the slow revolving fields, the speeding train, and the leaping song of excitement in my heart.

I took out my gun-metal watch which I had won at the fair. It was attached to a heavy imitation silver chain, with links so large and cumbersome that when the boys at school first saw it they called me 'Convict 99.' With my watch I timed the speed of the train by a method my father had shown me. At every quarter of a mile along the railway line was a small post with fractions of a mile painted on it. You made a note of the time that the train took to run between one post and the next and then worked out the number of miles an hour the train was travelling. When I worked it out the train appeared to be travelling at seventy miles an hour. I never was very good at arithmetic. However, it was nice to think that the train might be travelling at this speed; it would be something to boast about when I returned home.

Our luggage had gone on in advance and my mother intended to cross London in a cab. But a kindly porter put us on a bus which passed the station. 'No need to waste your money, lady,' he said. My mother gave him sixpence and the porter touched his hat.

On the bus a lady in front of us asked the conductor the best way to get to a certain street. The conductor gave her very full and definite directions.

'What a wonderful memory you have,' said the lady.

'Yes, mum,' said the conductor, 'I 've got a wonderful memory—always have had a wonderful memory. I won a prize for it at school, but I forget what it was.'

After crossing London we changed to the South Eastern and Chatham line (the Slow, Easy, and Comfortable, my father called it). I was too tired to continue my sightseeing and fell asleep. I awoke at a station to hear heavy footsteps overhead and the rattle of oil lamps. A man was plodding along the roof of the train to fix lamps in each compartment. It was now dark and when I alighted on the platform the comparatively bright lamps of the station sent little wavy lines of light into my eyes.

We drove through the quiet streets of the town and I craned my head out of the cab to watch the lighted windows of the shops. For the first time I saw electric lamps. True I had seen big arc-lamps at the fair at home, but these small domesticated ones looked snug and cosy like imprisoned glow-worms crawling round the insides of windows. The balls of glowing filament seemed to me a greater magic than the familiar incandescent gas mantle.

There was a street lamp outside my uncle's house also miraculously lit by electricity, and by its illumination I saw above the small many-paned shop-window the inscription: 'Theodore Barnes—Baker.'

Then the front door opened and the narrow passage between the bakehouse and the shop appeared to be full of people. My uncle seized my hand and ruffled my hair; my Aunt Ada greeted my mother and kissed me at the same time; Aunt Martha, her roly-poly face creased with an emotion betwixt laughter and tears, drew me from rival embraces and rapidly bestowed moist kisses all over my cheeks. After the quiet, unemotional atmosphere of my home, this almost rabid demonstration of affection was not unwelcome. When the grown-ups had ceased embracing, I became aware of my two cousins, a girl of about my own age, who smiled at me shyly, and her little sister of seven, who danced up and down, crying softly: 'He's come, he's come, the little boy is here.'

During the first three days at my uncle's house it rained and I was confined indoors. I did not mind this in the least, because I was able to romp with my cousins up and down the passage and stairs and in and out of the rooms to my heart's content. The long passage downstairs ran from the front door to the living-room at the back. Down this passage we raced at speed. It was so narrow that we were able to bounce our bodies against the walls, from side to side, and it became our special delight to throw ourselves sideways at a point midway so that we might go spinning through the open doorway into the tiny parlour that occupied a snug space behind the shop.

The reactions of the grown-ups to our noisy game were characteristic. My Aunt Ada uttered plaintive admonitory cries, fearful of damage to the furniture; Aunt Martha was concerned that we might injure ourselves; while my uncle surprised me by entering into the game—shouting and whooping and generally egging us on to even wilder displays of frenzy. Growing bolder I extended the radius of my operations to the shop door and even into the shop itself. This was my uncle's special domain. Here, immaculate in his white coat and baker's cap, he would add up his accounts, serve a customer, or interview a traveller. At my precipitate entry I expected to see his smiling face change expression, assume a frowning displeasure —but no, as I rushed past him pursued by my cousins, his mobile features extended his smile to a wide grin. He produced from some unknown quarter a long wooden pudding-spoon and gave chase, using his weapon to spank my behind as I clambered for safety over sacks of flour that stood in a corner of the shop.

At this moment my Aunt Ada put her head round the door to announce dinner. 'Really, Theodore,' she exclaimed, glancing at my uncle with an expression of comic helplessness, 'you are as bad as the children!'

Quite unabashed my uncle drove us before him down the passage to the living-room, where we scrambled for places round the table. It was very warm in here, for in addition to a fire in the grate the bakehouse oven backed on to the inside wall of the room. The wall was hot to the touch and provided a meeting-place for innumerable flies which crawled aimlessly up and down the wallpaper. Hitherto I had been impregnated with the idea that flies were wicked creatures, wholly devoted to the spreading of unpleasant germs, but in this amazingly delightful household they passed unnoticed, contributing a thin background of sound against the loud chatter of human voices.

At last we were seated. My uncle sat just inside the door in order that he might get out quickly if summoned by the shop-bell. This door was usually kept open because of the heat, but we were so crowded that it was necessary to leave it partly closed, to give space for my uncle's chair. I was given a seat next to him and he superintended my needs, pressing food upon me with great gusto. When a plate of meat was passed to me by my aunt from the other end of the table, he pretended to be horrified at the smallness of the amount.

'What are you trying to do?' he cried. 'Starve the boy?'

Meanwhile Aunt Martha, who had an inordinate love of pepper, had taken an overdose and was now sneezing and coughing vigorously. Uncle Theo at once joined in with a loud 'snashum!'

'Must have taken too much pepper,' he said between paroxysms. He nudged me with his elbow and said: 'What about you?' I quickly took the hint, my cousins also, and soon we were all sneezing in unison, my uncle producing veritable thunderclaps of sound easily heard above the rest.

My uncle loved the sights and sounds of his native place, and to take a walk with him through the town was to receive an education in minutiae. Nothing escaped his notice. Any alteration to shop fronts or houses received his attention and excited his comment.

'I see old So-and-so has had his house painted,' he said, as we stood opposite a neighbour's dwelling. 'Don't think much of the colour. Too bright. Will fade in no time. Cost him a pretty penny, I'll be bound. Wonder who got the job.'

Presently we came to a pork-butcher's shop. 'Got to go in here,' said Uncle Theo, 'for a pound of usages.' I stared at him. 'There it is,' he said, laughing at my bewilderment. 'Look on the window.' White enamel letters were stuck on the glass forming three words. Originally they read Best Pork Sausages, but the two first letters of the word sausages had fallen off. When he had purchased the sausages we returned home by way of a side street that led through the residential part of the town, and my uncle enlivened the occasion with descriptions of the people who lived there.

'See that house,' he said; 'that's where old Coffin lives. Takes snuff. Took too big a dose one day and sneezed so violently he rupt—well, he strained himself.'

A little later we came to a big gloomy-looking dwelling with cracked window-sills and sun-blistered paint. 'That's old Moffit's house. Moved in there a month ago. Used to live over his shop. Spent his savings to buy this. Got to keep a servant to run it. Nasty draughty-looking place. Next thing you know he'll be trying to sell it.'

There was no rancour in my uncle's remarks. He was well able to afford a private house of his own; indeed, his family sometimes suggested the idea, but he preferred living where he was over the shop. He was snug and happy there and saw no point in spending money to be made uncomfortable. 'Yes,' he would say, when the idea of moving was put forward, 'let's spend all our money on a grand house. We can sleep in a different room each night and live on bread and cheese.'

Before my Uncle Theodore took a walk he would spend a considerable time in his room changing and getting ready.   If the getting ready took over an hour we knew that something special and unusual was going to happen.   On one such occasion I looked into his room and saw him walking about in his shirt-sleeves. He always left the door of his room open so that he could move quickly and freely in and out, for in addition to dressing he carried on other activities at the same time.   These subsidiary activities were chiefly concerned with money, which he kept in various parts of the house.   There was money in the shop till and on a shelf in the corner of the shop where he kept reserve coppers and odd threepenny pieces in a jam-jar. There was also money in the parlour—some of it in a cash-box and some in a vase on the mantelshelf, and not infrequently piles of coins could be seen on a small table under the window which Uncle Theo used as a desk for writing business correspondence.

But the main repository or bank was his bedroom, where on a tall chest of drawers my uncle stacked and paraded columns of coin of every unit and denomination.

He was examining and counting these coins when I looked in.

'Hallo, Norman, come in,' he said.   He waved his left hand absently in my direction and with his right jotted down some figures in a note-book.   I went in and sat down on a chair.   My uncle finished his calculations, crossed to the mirror and began to insert a bow tie under his collar.   He was wearing a pair of French grey trousers beautifully pressed and creased. Coat and waistcoat to match lay ready to hand on the bed.   Uncle Theo commenced to tie the tie, then suddenly took it off.   'Not a very good match,' he said.   'Let 's try something else.'

He went back to the money on the chest of drawers. He moved the silver into a different position, studied the result for a moment, then put the lot into a drawer.

He recrossed the room, opened a cupboard, and took out a pair of brown shoes. 'Need a shine,' he said. They looked spotless to me, but my uncle rubbed them vigorously with a velvet pad. This accomplished he went downstairs to fetch his cash-box, opened the drawer and put the money into the box. 'That's that,' he said. He opened another drawer and took out a black tie with white spots. When he had tied this he inspected it critically in the glass to his evident satisfaction. He next put on his waistcoat and pulled it down front and back, examining the result in the mirror by a succession of frontal and side glances. He brushed his hair, twirled the ends of his moustache, and finally put on his coat. Next he took down a round box from the top of the cupboard, opened it, and produced a grey felt hat. This he carefully brushed with a narrow hat-brush, employing long steady strokes. He placed the hat on his head, adjusted it at a slight angle, ran his finger round the front of the brim, and then took it off and placed it gently on the bed. He crossed the room, put his head out of the door and shouted: 'All ready down there? Train goes at three twenty-five.'

My Aunt Ada came quickly out of the living-room. 'Why, Theo,' she exclaimed, 'that only leaves us twenty minutes! You didn't say we were going out.'

My uncle withdrew his head into the room and turned to me. 'Hurry up,' he said. 'Time you got ready. Want to look smart when you go to the sea-side, you know.'

I dashed out of the room and met my mother coming up the stairs. Down below there was the sound of confused voices and people rushing about. For the next few minutes pandemonium reigned. The narrow stairs, scarcely wider than two feet across, became a bottle-neck through which Aunt Ada, Aunt

*D

Martha, and my two cousins tried to pass at the same time to get to their respective rooms. Meanwhile Uncle Theo stood calmly in his room giving his hat a final brush.

It did not seem possible that we should be ready in time to catch the train, but somehow we were. My uncle led the way through the town, saying: 'Plenty of time—no need to rush.' He even paused a moment to examine a new sun-blind outside a stationer's shop and congratulate the proprietor, who was standing in the doorway. When we reached the station the train was in. The guard raised his flag—we stumbled into the nearest compartment and the train started on its journey.

My aunt and uncle held a party in celebration of our visit. Uncle Theodore's brother Robert arrived with his wife and two daughters, Eva and Maud. My Uncle Robert was a big broad-shouldered man, kindly and jovial. He had a magnificent moustache, and when he laughed the hairs of his moustache danced and waved about like a field of corn beneath the wind. His wife Evelyn was dark, plump, and rather reserved. My two cousins, Eva and Maud, were in their early twenties and had the dark complexion of their mother.

Uncle Robert came swinging down the passage and greeted me boisterously. 'Hallo, my boy! How are you?' he cried. Then before I could reply, he slapped a piece of paper into my hand saying: 'My card.' It was a postal order for ten shillings. 'You must put part of that in your money-box,' said my mother. 'Always do what your mother tells you,' said Uncle Robert, 'and you won't go far wrong. But all the same your uncle says spend it. Buy some sweets and have a good cram.'

The centre of the party, the still space which is said to be in the middle of every whirlpool, was the parlour, now filled to overflowing. Chairs had been pushed back against the walls and all were occupied. More people continued to arrive and were obliged to stay in the passage or stand round the door of the living-room. One of my cousins sat on the piano stool and singing was started. My Aunt Ada sang and then my mother, followed by Maud and Eva.

'Hark at the song-birds warbling,' said Uncle Theo. He was full of vitality, moving nimbly about in the confined space, joking and laughing with every one and distributing fruit, nuts, and sweets. He produced a box of cigars, and soon he and Uncle Robert were puffing vigorously.

During a pause in the singing my mother said to Maud and Eva: 'And when are you two fine girls going to get married?'

'Now don't encourage them, Aunt Cathy,' said Uncle Robert, giving his booming laugh.

'I shouldn't think they need much encouragement,' said my mother.

'Oh, auntie!' cried Maud happily. 'What things you do say!'

The smoke from the cigars drifted to the ceiling and eddied through the open doorway. The people in the passage pressed to the edge of the room to watch and hear the singers. First I saw one face and then another. One moment a face would be there and then it would seem to fade away with the tobacco smoke, disappearing slowly from view like the cat in *Alice in Wonderland*.

Sandwiches, pies, and sausage-rolls were passed round, followed by plates of jelly and blancmange. I saw Uncle Theo bend down in a corner of the room and fumble in a cupboard, from which he produced a bottle of wine. He filled glasses and toasts were proposed. I felt rather shy and self-conscious while all this was going on, for I was unused to exuberance on this scale and the toasts, given with an air of great earnestness and solemnity, made me wonder if there was something I ought to do to contribute to the ritual.

But presently singing started again and amid cries of encouragement Uncle Theo was persuaded to sing his special song. It had a lively tune and its theme was money—not the money of the banks and big business, but the friendly, near-to-hand money of the trousers pocket. I cannot remember the words, except that the chorus contained a great deal about 'chink, chink, chink,' during the singing of which my uncle rattled the loose change in his pockets and danced up and down the room twisting and twirling his legs in a most professional manner.

This song was the climax of the party and very soon afterwards people began to go home. For this I was not sorry. My eyelids were drooping and I had a most uncomfortable feeling at the pit of my stomach. In fact, a short while later I disgraced the evening by being sick in my bedroom.

Towards the end of our stay with Uncle Theo my father joined us. The town in which my Uncle Theo lived was also my father's birthplace and it was here that he had met my mother and married her.

His father had been a miller, his mill a windmill. The mill had since changed hands, but was still working, so my father took me out to see it. It stood on high ground about a mile from the town. We crossed the railway line by a footbridge and climbed up forty steps cut into the side of the cliff. When we reached the top we saw the mill about a quarter of a mile away. The nearer we approached the taller it seemed to grow. It was built almost entirely of wood and stood on a stone base. Round the lower part of the wooden structure was a sort of veranda above which the great sails, or sweeps as they were called locally, were slowly revolving. The sails were composed of wooden slats, something like the slats of a Venetian blind, which opened in varying degrees according to the strength of the wind. The top of the mill, to which the four sails were attached, moved round like a turn-table so that the sails always faced the wind.

As I watched the sweeps slowly slicing the air I thought of the episode in *Don Quixote*, when the dauntless knight charged the windmill, mistaking it for an adversary. I understood, too, why the episode was a favourite one with my father.

We went inside and saw the corn being crushed between the heavy millstones. Not until that moment had I realized the significance of the phrase 'the upper and nether millstone'; or appreciated to the full the biblical quotation, 'It were better for him that a millstone were hanged about his neck, and he cast into the sea.'

When the day came for our departure my heart was heavy and sad. I did not want to go home. At no other place had the sun the same friendly touch as here; the very air was gay and intoxicating, even the whistles of distant trains had a special magic all their own.

My uncle, aunts, and cousins crowded the doorway to see us off. It seemed but a short time since I had arrived and tumbled into their affectionate, welcoming arms, and now I would not see them again for a long time. I suppose I pulled a long face, for Uncle Theo seemed to be mocking me. His features were drawn in melancholy. I thought it unfeeling of him to tease me at such a time. I gave him a short indignant push and now I saw that there were tears in his eyes. He uttered a queer half-suppressed sob and suddenly I realized that he was really weeping. I was immediately contrite, ashamed of myself and my petulance; but I was so surprised to see a grown-up giving way to such obvious and noisy emotion that I did not know what to say or do.

We climbed into the waiting cab and it set off for the station. As we rounded the corner into the main road I saw Uncle Theo raise his handkerchief to his eyes, then he waved it violently in our direction. All day as we travelled homewards I retained in my mind the picture of this lovable emotional man with the tears running down his cheeks with unashamed abandon.

CHAPTER XVII

SCHOOL SPORTS AND ELEANOR

My preparatory school was situated at the bottom of a hill, beyond which a slow gentle river wandered contentedly through green pasture lands. In this pleasant valley there stood the house of a lady of wealth and distinction. From the school playground we could see the 'big house,' as it was called, standing away to the north on a rising slope of close-cropped grass. On either side of the wide Georgian house an avenue of trees formed leafy wings that half enclosed the lawns and gardens of the estate beyond the water meadows. The lady of the big house showed a friendly and benevolent interest in the school and at the end of the summer term she permitted the use of her grounds for our school sports. There were no lessons on the last day of term and the morning was spent by the boys in preparing for the events of the afternoon. Chairs, folding tables, benches, ropes, stakes, and other miscellaneous paraphernalia were carried from the school through a private door in the wall of the estate and deposited in the marquee tent erected each year for refreshments and prize-giving.

We were usually fortunate in having fine weather for the occasion and some of my happiest moments were spent on those sunny mornings making the journey from school to sports field with a chair in my arms or a bundle of wooden stakes over my shoulder. I would pause on my way and stand on the bridge that spanned the river to watch the smooth water sliding silently beneath me, or look across the smiling vale at the distant hills, between which the river ran in wide sweeping curves through fields of glimmering buttercups. Those mornings of preparation held for me a greater appeal than the events themselves, which usually followed a prescribed routine during which I was kept constantly busy with no time to stand and stare.

At the end of my last summer term our sports day was again favoured with brilliant sunshine. I was now fifteen years old and my parents had decided to send me to a boarding school for the next two years, so as one of the senior boys of my preparatory school I was expected to set an example on my last day by entering for as many events as possible.

The sports began at three-thirty and I plodded my way dutifully through the long jump, the high jump, the hundred yards, and the mile race. During the interval I sat on the grass next to one of the older boys who, like myself, was spending his last day at school.

'I hear you are down for a prize, Hancock,' he said. This was news to me.

'A prize for what?' I inquired.

'Can't say. General excellence or something of the kind, I should imagine. Looks nice when you are leaving and it's an advertisement for the school.'

So saying the cynic stood up and wandered away to the refreshment tent.

This information was as unexpected as it was pleasant and filled me with a warm anticipatory glow. The afternoon was nearly over. As usual I had made but a poor performance on the sports field, but now I had something to look forward to. One more event, namely the tug-of-war, was to take place and then tea would be served. By some happy coincidence the team on my end of the rope proved victorious. The two sides were evenly matched and it was some time before the contest was determined in our favour. Though I dug my feet into the ground and tugged and sweated, I cannot think my efforts had much to do with the result, unless in flattery my contribution can be compared to the proverbial straw. Somewhat dizzy from my exertions I looked around and found myself gazing directly at a girl a few years older than myself, who stood among the spectators. She was dressed in a dark skirt and a white silk blouse. About her shoulders hung a navy-blue cape, joined at the neck by a scarlet cord. Perched on her head was a velvet tam-o'-shanter, beneath which her jet-black hair hung in heavy folds.

The thought ran through my mind, I am glad she saw me on the winning side. Then I blushed. The girl was smiling at me, and I noticed that my parents were standing next to the stranger. With them was Mr. Carlton, the editor of our local paper. My mother was waving to me. I think she had been trying to attract my attention for some time, for as I walked towards the group I saw her turn to her friends and say something which set them laughing.

When I came up to them my mother said: 'This is Eleanor, Mr. Carlton's niece.' We shook hands and Mr. Carlton said: 'We usually call her Ellen—then she does not feel too important.'

'I never feel important,' replied Ellen, and added with a twinkle: 'Except when I am staying with editors.'

We walked towards the trees, where tables had been set up for tea. The sun had started its downward course. Undiminished in power, its rays filtered through the upper foliage of the trees and spattered the crowd sitting round the tables with sequins of light that fell upon heads and shoulders like luminous confetti.

It was my job to hand round sandwiches and cakes

and for the next ten minutes I was kept busy journey-
ing to and from the refreshment tent. When I returned to the table to make a hurried meal I found
that Mr. Carlton and my father had gone for a stroll.
My mother was chatting with a lady of her acquaintance
and Eleanor Carlton was talking to the boy who earlier
had spoken to me about my being down for a prize.
I hoped he had said nothing to her about this. I did
not like to ask her the question point-blank, and in
my attempt to avoid one kind of clumsiness I fell into
another.

I said abruptly: 'Do you know that boy?'

She made no reply, but instead began to talk of books
and writing. She asked me if I liked poetry and spoke
of some verses she had contributed to a school magazine.
She spoke of books as if they were living things and not
text-books or classics immobilized behind glass doors.
My mind kindled to her enthusiasm. She spoke with
a vitality that was contagious and I found myself ex-
pressing opinions which sprang up in my mind in full
and unexpected maturity. I forgot the people around
us. We seemed to be enclosed in a brilliant iridescent
bubble, which muted the sounds of voices and tea-cups.
Although I had decided to omit all reference to the
forthcoming prize-giving, the subject seemed to swim
into our conversation of its own volition. Ellen, it
appeared, had no great opinion of prizes. The main
thing was to attempt achievement; the extent of its
success could not be measured by the giving or with-
holding of rewards. This revolutionary idea was
readily accepted by me. As a potential prize-winner
I could afford to show a careless indifference to the
spoils of endeavour.

Presently I became aware of a sudden distracting
silence. Tea was over and parents and boys had taken
their seats in front of the large marquee tent, in the

opening of which, protected from the sun, was a low platform occupied by the head master and his friends. Ellen and I joined the others and took up a position in the last row of chairs. Ellen seemed quite unperturbed by the fact that we had missed the opening speech by the lady of the big house. As we sat down the head master began to call out the names of the prize-winners. I assumed what I hoped was an attitude of bland detachment, but in actual fact I felt a combination of suppressed excitement and nervous apprehension at the prospect of walking up to the platform to make my bow.

Ellen was amused at the performance of the prize-winners as they received their gifts. Some bent stiffly forward and stuck out their behinds as though going through the first motions of a gymnastic exercise. Others jerked their heads quickly without giving their bodies a chance to co-operate. I found nothing funny in their awkward posturings, for each bowing figure in front of me was the ghost of myself in rehearsal. Slowly the headmaster approached the end of the list without mentioning my name, and then suddenly he had finished and was making his closing speech. I suppose I looked disappointed, for Ellen gave me an encouraging smile as if to say 'You are well out of that.'

My parents and Mr. Carlton joined us and we started for home. We had taken only a few steps when I heard my name called. I turned round and met the headmaster hurrying towards me.

'So sorry,' he said, 'your name was overlooked. There are a few books left, however, and you can take your choice.' I walked with him to the platform. On a table were four books. The headmaster picked up one and handed it to me. 'How about this?' he said.

I felt in no mood to discriminate and said: 'Thank you, sir.' I put the book under my arm and walked

away. Before I rejoined my parents I glanced at the
title. The book was *The Lances of Lynwood* by
Charlotte M. Yonge. There was no inscription
inside, so the precise nature of my scholastic accomplishment remained undisclosed. My 'excellence'
could hardly have been more 'general.'

I saw a great deal of Ellen during the rest of the
summer holiday, but I rarely recaptured the easy
intimacy of our first meeting. Sometimes we sat
together in the garden at Cornhill House, on the rustic
seat beneath the pear-tree, and read the same book.
The sunlight dappled the pages; my eyes followed the
printed words, my mind unreceptive to their meaning.
In a trance-like state I was conscious of Ellen's
proximity; the slow rise and fall of her breast, the
movement of her hair beneath the eddying summer
breeze.

Sometimes we took walks together through the green
cloistered lanes. Ellen spoke of pictures and plays she
had seen, discussed politics, personalities, and movements. I knew next to nothing of these things and
could make no response. I longed to be witty, in-
telligent, and entertaining, but remained dumb or at
best achieved only a stammering incoherency of phrase.
My words seemed as empty and void as the vast
expanse of cloudless sky which extended above us
from horizon to horizon in arched irony. In an
attempt to express intensity of feeling and perception
I made silly little remarks, feeble clichés of inexact
observation about the beauty of the countryside.

We discussed too metaphysical subjects, propound-
ing such questions as the difference between altruism
and love; was mankind innately selfish? What was the
highest form and manifestation of love? Was Shelley
right when he asserted that the most disinterested and

spiritual love was the love a sister bears towards a sister?

In these speculations I became more vocal, delighted in the belief that I had discovered new aspects of truth. Such was my innocence of emotional development that I imagined my newly awakened ardour was aroused by the excitement of discussion.

When Ellen returned home at the conclusion of her holiday, I felt intensely lonely. I walked the familiar lanes in a mood of bitter-sweet melancholy—confused and helpless in my immaturity.

CHAPTER XVIII

TRADE OR PROFESSION?

I LEFT school when I was seventeen years old with no very clear idea of what I wanted to do to earn a living. My obvious course under these circumstances was to become apprenticed to the drapery trade with the ultimate intention of entering my father's business. But the obvious is seldom attractive. Youth is inclined to dispute the advice of Charles Kingsley to 'do the work that's nearest'—nor could I find any consolation in Patmore's dictum: 'Our solace is, the sad road lies so clear.'

My mother, kindest of women, sensing my indecision, said: 'Perhaps you would like to be a chemist?' I was supposed to be good at chemistry, because a phrenologist after feeling my bumps had declared that I showed a marked aptitude for science. 'Or a traveller,' continued my mother; and for a moment I had visions of exploration and foreign lands. But I was soon undeceived.

'You would start first in the wholesale,' said my mother, 'and after a time they would send you out with samples.'

I remained silent, trying to picture myself in the role of the voluble gentlemen I had heard speaking to my father in the shop.

'I think you would do very well as a commercial traveller,' said my mother, with admirable persistence. 'After all, you have a money-making nose.'

I felt my nose. It was certainly big, but I was dubious of its acquisitive ability. Instinctively I was aware that I lacked the commercial sense and that to acquire it I must do violence to my nature. Ambition to succeed was reckoned a cardinal virtue in the world of my upbringing. And by success was meant the acquisition of money and possessions. I did not object to these things; on the contrary, it was difficult at my age, living in moderately comfortable circumstances, to imagine life without them. But I felt that my path lay in some other direction than that of commerce. Yet what direction? Here I came up against the opaque wall of my restricted vision, my lack of talent, and my ignorance as to the nature of other and suitable methods of earning a livelihood.

At the back of my mind I had a vague idea that I might be able to earn a living by writing. The only subject at school in which I had displayed a moderate ability was the writing of essays. So now I put forward the suggestion that I might become a journalist.

After further discussion in which we went round in a circle and came back to the same place, or moved off at a tangent and arrived nowhere, my father, who hitherto had remained silent, said: 'Well, if you want to be a journalist you had better go up to London and have a look at Fleet Street.' He mentioned the name of a friend who edited a small technical journal. 'Go up and see Gregory Warren,' said my father, 'and he will tell you all about it and you will get some idea of what journalism is like.'

I journeyed up to London with a feeling of adventure in my heart. I left my bag in the small family hotel, where a room had been booked for me, and then set out to pay my visit to Mr. Warren. His office was on the fifth floor of a block of buildings situated in a maze of narrow streets between Fleet Street and the Embankment. In the lobby of the building was a lift, which people worked themselves without the assistance of an attendant. I never have liked machinery and this particular piece of machinery had a sort of malignant look about it. There was something faintly sinister about a cage which could be set in motion at the operation of an invisible agent. As I entered the building the lift was descending; it settled itself down with a jaunty bounce and seemed to give me a black stare. I touched the gate gingerly and was about to slide it open when the cage trembled and moved upwards out of sight. I turned away, rather thankful to the lift for its desertion, and climbed the stone stairs. I walked along a corridor and discovered the name of the paper edited by Mr. Warren on a glass door. I pushed open the door, entered briskly, and almost collided with a wooden counter. This counter formed two sides of a square, so small that I felt like a prisoner standing in a dock. From somewhere in the gloomy recesses of the room a youth slid from a high stool and stood silently confronting me. I asked if Mr. Warren were in and the youth said: 'Name?' I gave my name and with a backward nod of the head the youthful monosyllabic attendant motioned me to enter. I lifted the flap of the counter and went through into the inner office. Mr. Warren rose to greet me. He was a short man with grey hair and grey, tired eyes. He spoke to me kindly, but with an air of abstraction.

'So you want to be a journalist,' he said, smiling. The smile softened his features, but the tired withdrawn look in his eyes remained. 'I've got to go out,' he continued, 'so suppose we walk along the Embankment and find a seat in the gardens where we can have a talk.'

Walking beside Mr. Warren made me feel part of London. I was intrigued by the sights and sounds about me—the sun glinting on the wide waters of the river, the twinkle and clang of the gliding, lolloping trams, and the people walking quickly in every direction. The impetuous gush and roar of London, its vibrant, sparkling air, intoxicated me so that I was only half conscious of what Mr. Warren was saying. One remark he made brought me to earth with a jolt. He made an inquiry about my parents and I said that they were shortly taking a holiday.

'A holiday,' he said, in his flat, measured voice. 'I 've not had a holiday for twenty years.'

We found a seat in the gardens opposite a bandstand. Folding chairs were stacked against the pillars that supported the roof of the stand, and from the roof hung pots of geraniums. The scarlet blooms glowed in the sunlit air like petals of flame. Behind us towered tall triumphant buildings, whose massive cliff-like walls seemed as impervious to the passing of time as they were contemptuous of the trickle of humanity that crawled beneath them.

By an effort of will I turned from the contemplation of my surroundings to listen to what Mr. Warren was saying. He recounted for my benefit his early experiences as a journalist. There was a sadness in his voice which belied the beauty of the scene before me, and I was so carried away with the sheer delight of living that how I was to earn my bread appeared at this moment of little importance. Yet in spite of my excitement there was somewhere inside me, like the cold jewel centred within the feverish activities of a watch, a hard core of realism. I knew that when this elation of the spirit had passed, sombre truth would once more come into its own.

'Your father has established a successful business,' said Mr. Warren, 'and you would be foolish to throw away a settled career for the hazardous pursuits of journalism.'

There was truth in Mr. Warren's advice and—I

was forced to admit—little glamour in his manner of living. And so I returned home a potential draper. Writing must wait upon the fortunes of commerce. In the meanwhile I would call to my aid patience, the beggar's only virtue.

Now that I had made up my mind—or rather had it made up for me—events moved quickly. Within a month I was apprenticed to a draper in a large town near London. The apprenticeship ran for two years and cost my father forty pounds, which was repaid to me as pocket-money during the period of my employment.

CHAPTER XIX

I BECOME AN APPRENTICE

WALKING from the station through the business section of the town, I approached the shop that was to be my home for the next two years. In one hand I carried a new umbrella, in the other a shabby Gladstone bag. I was wearing my best clothes—a double-breasted navy suit modelled in style on my father's, navy socks with purple clocks, and a bowler hat.

The shop was situated on a corner of the main street; its high plate glass windows, the shine and glitter of its fittings, and the imposing gold-lettered sign which extended across the shop front like an ornate watch-chain across a prosperous stomach, presented to my youthful eye a resplendent magnificence. I could not imagine myself a servitor in this palace of commerce, and my misgiving was further increased by the discovery that the only entrance to the living quarters was through the shop itself. For a moment I paused in hesitation. Placing my belongings on the pavement, I took off my hat and mopped my brow. Then taking my courage, together with my bag and umbrella, in both hands I entered. At once the 'dry-goods' smell so familiar to me at Cornhill House assailed my nostrils, the smell of cotton and wool materials stacked in fixtures and cases or displayed in mountainous heaps upon stands and counters. There was also another, more aristocratic, odour inextricably mixed with the familiar—an odour which emanated from silks, satins, and velvets hung enticingly from brass ceiling rails. The warm colours of these rich stuffs made a glowing background to the rows of heads, both male and female, which seemed to be turned in my direction from behind mahogany counters.

Somewhat bedazzled, I kept my eye upon the door of an office at the extreme end of the shop and was about to advance in this direction when a young man appeared from behind a pile of cotton prints and, with a note of inquiry in his voice, spoke my name. Upon my admitting my identity, he introduced himself as Stacey, my fellow apprentice, whose room I was to share. He became my mentor and guide and I followed him between the aisles of shining counters to the frozen-faced glass door of the office. In the office I was introduced to my employer who, with a few kind words, put me at my ease. When I had received a general description of my duties, Stacey made an opportune reappearance and conducted me to my room. As we climbed the stairs I was able—now that my nervousness had somewhat abated—to give him my full attention. His face was oval, his expression open—the eyes wide and innocent. Fair corn-coloured hair, which grew low on his forehead and was brushed back over his head in long, wavy folds, gave to him the appearance of a good-tempered faun. I had little experience of my fellows and was unable to assess character at a glance, but instinct persuaded me that in Stacey I had found a friend. In short I took a liking to him at once and he in turn was kindly disposed towards me. It was, perhaps, an attraction of opposites, for he was confident, carefree, and full of buoyant exuberance, while I in contrast was a tightly nerved introspective creature, hopeful and idealistic, but unsure of myself.

The room that I shared with Stacey was situated at the top of the house. A Frenchman once wrote a book entitled *A Journey round my Room*. There was no need for me to make a journey round mine. I could see all that it contained from a stationary position. There were two beds, a chest of drawers, a washstand, a chair, and a full-length mirror. This mirror dominated the room. Once it had occupied a place of importance in a millinery department. Now in old age, its glass blotched and stained like the face of an elderly roué, it still retained, in spite of infirmity, a certain brash distinction. It tilted backwards or forwards as required, but the springs had long since gone and now the glass had to be propped into position with a wedge of paper. Sometimes the paper fell out and I would see the reflection of my body fall violently backwards as though in a faint, or propelled forwards as if attacked from behind.

This glass was an uncomfortable companion, a candid friend that never tired of bringing to my notice unpalatable truths.

Hitherto when I shaved, which fortunately was only twice a week, I had used a small mirror which gave me a tiny or partial view of my face. But this larger mirror was unequivocal, it asserted its truths boldly; and when I looked into it and met its scrofulous stare I saw behind the pock-marked surface of the glass my face in its entirety—a long sallow face with large earnest eyes, bushy jet-black hair, a long straight nose, and a slightly cleft chin. As I moved about the room dressing or undressing, I would catch a glimpse of my reflection fatuously copying my every move, and when I stood still, half turned from the glass, I would observe with shocking clarity my short neck, rather hunched shoulders, and projecting ears.

In addition to Stacey and myself there were eight men employed on the staff. Two were shopwalkers and the rest were evenly divided between the Manchester and dress departments.   The two shopwalkers, who, unlike the rest of us, lived out, were the 'officers' of the business and controlled the activities of the staff. Mr. Brown, the senior shopwalker, arrived each morning at seven-thirty.   Stacey and I were supposed to be up and dressed at this hour ready to sweep out the shop, but we were usually late.

Mr. Brown had the voice and appearance of the old type of sergeant-major, but we were not intimidated by his loud voice and startling language.   Every one in the shop knew that Mr. Brown hid a soft heart beneath his brusque manner, and since neither Stacey nor myself enjoyed early rising, we had no compunction in taking advantage of his good nature.

Stacey had perfected a system of rapid dressing which enabled him to make his appearance downstairs within a few minutes of Mr. Brown's arrival. His wardrobe for these occasions was reduced to a minimum and consisted of shirt, trousers, coat, and a pair of elastic-sided shoes.   If time permitted, and he was in a more formal mood, he added a collar and stud bow.   (A stud bow is a ready-made bow with a stud which can be fastened into position between the wings of the collar.)   His shirt, trousers, and coat hung on a row of pegs behind the door and when he heard Mr. Brown's voice bellowing threats and objurgations up the stairs, he went into immediate action.   With one bound he leapt from his bed and hurled himself at the suspended garments.   Only the slow-motion camera could do justice to his manner of dressing. At one moment there was a flurry of whirling clothes and the next instant he was dressed.   Such methods were not for me.   I soon realized that I could not compete with my fellow apprentice in his time-defying act, and made a point of rising before him.

When we entered the shop Stacey presented a bright

and innocent face to Mr. Brown and wished him a respectful 'Good morning.'

'You are late, Stacey,' said Mr. Brown.

'Sorry, sir. I overslept a little. Went to book-keeping class last night.'

This was Stacey's standard excuse and the book-keeping class became a standard joke. It was true that Stacey did attend such a class, but no one succeeded in discovering on what particular night it was held. Stacey, when pressed, asserted that the nights were constantly changed to meet the convenience of individual pupils.

I started my duties in the Manchester department, where I was put to work dusting and tidying the fixtures, fetching and carrying, sorting tickets, running errands, and making myself generally useful. If a piece of calico or other material was required from reserve stock, it was my job to go down and fetch it from the basement. The basement, or cellar, ran in a series of galleries under the shop and was illuminated by two or three blear-eyed electric lamps. When business was quiet Stacey and I were sent down to 'squad up' the fixtures, or to make an inventory of their contents. The woollen blankets were kept down here and on one occasion Stacey climbed on top of them and fell asleep. He was discovered thus by the 'governor,' who had taken it into his head to make an unannounced inspection. Stacey climbed down and said: 'I was testing the softness of the blankets, sir, and they were so comfortable I fell asleep.'

'I don't think you will find me quite so soft as the blankets, Stacey,' replied the governor, but he was obliged to turn away to hide a smile. There was something about Stacey—a combination of naïveté and adroitness—that was very engaging.

I enjoyed working behind the counter except when I had to serve a customer and then I was filled with confusion. I was so nervous that I could scarcely comprehend the simplest request. When the customer had made her choice and I had to cut off a length of material my scissors seemed unable to keep a straight line, and to hide my incompetence I indulged in rapid conversation on the state of the weather. Never, I imagine, had the vagaries of the weather been so thoroughly analysed and discussed. The amount or absence of sun, wind, rain, frost, hail, or snow, both during the past and present—and even in the future— were expounded by me from every conversational angle. To the staff—and especially to the women assistants—it became a joke. If one of the girls was going on an outing on early closing day, and was uncertain of the weather, someone was sure to say: 'Ask Hancock,' or 'Listen to Hancock the next time he serves a customer.'

My inefficiency as a salesman prompted me to take an interest in window-dressing. Mr. Camber was our chief window-dresser. A short dark man, he wore at all times a black morning coat and striped trousers. His moustache was waxed and pointed, and across his nose a pair of gold pince-nez glasses, balanced slightly off the horizontal, gave him a look of scholarly benevolence. It was fascinating to watch Mr. Camber at work, especially when engaged in dressing a 'fancy' window. This necessitated first the fixing of brass rods at varying levels to form a scaffolding upon which the goods were displayed. Then came the intricate task of hanging laces and ribbons in loops and folds over the rods with one end stuck to the glass of the window by a gum tab. It was customary to dress up close to the glass to produce the effect of variety and profusion. Between the laces Mr. Camber placed

gloves, scarves, collars, and cards of buttons, all
meticulously arranged at varying heights and depths.
It was my job to supply Mr. Camber with price
tickets. There were three kinds and shapes, namely
round, square, and what Mr. Camber called lozenge.
Thus, while I gazed at Mr. Camber's back until I
became lost in some pleasant reverie, I would be
jerked back to reality by Mr. Camber's voice as he
called out: 'One square 1s. 0¾d., two lozenge 1s. 6¾d.'
Sometimes he would ask for a descriptive ticket and I
would hand up an oblong of glazed cardboard bearing
the inscription 'Best Value,' 'Very Special,' or 'A
Bargain.' Mr. Camber was quite content to receive
any description I cared to select, for to the draper all
such descriptions are interchangeable.

As part of my training I was transferred for a period
to the dress department.

Certain animals adopt the coloration of their surroundings. Shop assistants too are influenced by
their environment. Men in the 'household linens'
are usually stolid and phlegmatic, but in the 'dresses'
the salesmen are more temperamental. They are
votaries in the temple of fashion; and the handling of
soft colourful fabrics seems to give them a lighter and
more imaginative outlook. When I was moved from
one department to the other I felt like one who emerges
from a dark wood into a flowering garden.

My reputation for 'weather talk' had preceded me
and Mr. Morgan, the handsome, curly-headed buyer
of the 'dresses,' welcomed me as 'Mr. Negretti.'
His colleagues, Mr. Corby and Mr. Reynolds, presented a striking contrast. Mr. Corby was the dandy
of the shop. He wore suits that were heavily braided.
Braid edged the revers of his double-breasted waistcoat and ran in a straight line down the seams of his

E

trousers. The pockets of his coat, also edged with braid, were cut on the slant to the shape of half-moons. He wore a high-wing collar and a cravat adorned with a pearl tie-pin. It was his proud boast that he never used the same collar twice.

Mr. Reynolds on the other hand was dressed in a plain black suit and a turn-down polo collar attached to a stiff white linen 'dicky.' He was a man of stern morality and principles. To him life was earnest. He neither smoked nor drank, but sometimes when he struggled to insert a stud through the implacable rigidity of his collar he would pronounce the word 'bother' with such vehemence that it sounded like the most terrible of oaths.

Mr. Morgan had a sense of humour which might perhaps be described as surrealist. One day Mr. Reynolds, after serving a man who had the reputation for crooked dealing, remarked sententiously: 'That man's hands are black with crime.'

Mr. Corby said, as though making a joke: 'They looked quite clean to me.'

'Yes,' said Mr. Morgan, 'he washes them in invisible ink.'

A frequent customer was a spinster lady who was very sanctimonious and gushing. She usually asked for something that was not in stock and when the assistant expressed his regret she would invariably exclaim: 'Oh dear! Oh dear!'

Mr. Morgan described her as being full of the 'oh dears of sanctity.'

Shop assistants at the time of my apprenticeship came from every stratum of society. I worked alongside men who had received a good education and others who had very little education at all; men who were the sons of farmers, parsons, clerks, and railway workers.

Shop assistants were, at this period, a migratory class moving from one place to another and often from one trade to another. One of my colleagues was an ex-sailor, another had worked in a factory, while yet another left the trade, attended college, and became a missionary. As a class shop assistants are generous to a fault. Like the members of the theatrical profession they will give their last penny to a comrade in difficulty. Once when I was short of money a touring company came to the town to present Shaw's *Man and Superman*. I had never seen a Shaw play and was greatly disappointed at the idea of having to miss this opportunity. I knew that Stacey had spent his salary and so had no hesitation in speaking to him of my disappointment, since, under the circumstances, my remarks could not be interpreted as a request for a loan.

Without saying anything to me, he rushed out that night, pawned his watch, and bought two tickets for the show. He insisted on coming to keep me company, although the play had no attractions for him—in fact he was terribly bored throughout the entire performance. This was typical. Whenever Stacey or I were hard up one or other of the seniors would come to our aid. Independence in money matters may be a virtue, but who could resist or resent such magnificent generosity?

The pay of a shop assistant was extremely low. Very few earned as much as two pounds a week, but the less they earned the more freely they spent. I rarely met a shop worker who saved; there was no such word as thrift in their vocabulary. They might be called counter-jumpers and white-collar wage-slaves, but in their manner of spending they were kings. Free, independent, and individualistic; they enjoyed their leisure hours to the full.

There were, of course, exceptions, especially among

shopwalkers. The shopwalker for one reason or another was inclined to remain for many years in one shop. Having reached middle age, he was perhaps fearful of change, afraid that he would be unable to adjust himself to different circumstances or newer methods of business. This was an age when men were spoken of as being too old at forty, and under the merciless lash of economic necessity such men would dye their hair, wear elastic-sided boots and even corsets, in a desperate attempt to preserve an illusion of vigour and youthfulness. As the years passed they grew more entrenched in their particular rut, until they became in old age soured and disgruntled time-servers who had only their servility and their record of faithfulness with which to bargain.

From my bedroom window I could hear the rumbling of the trams in the street and the hiss of the trolley poles on the singing wires. These sounds were associated in my mind with hot summer evenings, when, at the end of a long and trying day in the shop, I sat on the window-sill enjoying the feel of the air on my face. Stacey too would join me and we would sit scarcely exchanging a word and watch the light fade from the sky, until almost before we knew it the street lamps were alight and the chimney-pots on the roofs of the houses opposite stood black against the last lingering traces of daylight. Then, feeling hungry, we would go out and eat a meal of fish and chips at the fish shop, which was hidden away in an alley behind the main street. On other evenings Stacey took me with him to the music hall, theatre, or cinema, all new experiences for me, but neither of us was greatly enamoured of these diversions. We preferred to idle about in the streets and watch the crowds, or pass in and out of cafés to greet people we knew.

Stacey's weakness was for Dutch auction rooms. I went with him once to see what it was all about. The auction room was an empty shop, at the back of which the auctioneer, mounted on a table, harangued a small group of people in front of him. It was easy to see that Stacey was a favourite of the firm. At sight of him the auctioneer, whose habitual attitude towards his dumb congregation was one of contemptuous good humour, raised his voice and became even more eloquent and persuasive.

'Look closely at what I am offering you, ladies and gentlemen. Pass it round among you and examine it. You can see for yourselves what it is: a genuine self-filling, self-adjusting, gold-banded fountain-pen with a solid nine-carat gold nib of special strength and pliancy. Guaranteed for two years or your money returned. A pen like this will cost you fifteen shillings in your shops and stores. It would be amazingly cheap at ten shillings, an unheard-of bargain at seven and six. Now who will bid me five shillings for this pen? Let 's see if there is a man or woman of courage among you. Is any one here ready to speculate? Remember if you don't speculate you can't accumulate. What you don't put down you can't pick up. Will someone offer me five shillings for this remarkable pen which carries with it a two-year guarantee?'

The auctioneer paused and silence filled the shop.

'Very well, friends,' continued the auctioneer. 'I can see that I 've got a stubborn lot here to-night, but I 'll make you buy before I 've finished with you.' He turned to an assistant and said: 'Here, Joe, hand me up that inkstand from the shelf over there. Now, ladies and gentlemen, who will bid me five shillings for this pen and the inkstand?'

Stacey put up his hand.

'Thank you, sir,' said the auctioneer. 'Joe, take the gentleman's money.'

Stacey handed Joe the five shillings and the auctioneer continued: 'Now, sir, you have given me five shillings for this pen and inkstand. That's correct, is it not?'

Stacey nodded.

'Very well. Now just to show my gratitude to a man of perception and courage I am going to add to the lot you have just purchased this high-class compendium, containing fifty sheets of deckle - edged notepaper and envelopes to match. Here you are, Joe, give them to the gentleman with my compliments. And now, ladies and gentlemen, here is another pen of precisely similar make. Who will . . .' But we did not wait for more. Stacey was already on his way out with his purchases under his arm.

Stacey certainly had a way with him. Even to walk along the street in his company was an entertainment. He was so alive and so sure of himself. He swung along the pavement with an air. Under his arm he carried a black imitation malacca cane and on his head his straw hat was tilted at an angle.

He knew all the usual and unusual places where the youth of the town forgathered—billiards and ping-pong saloons, indoor fun fairs, a boxing booth where a black man challenged all comers; and an underground ice-cream parlour frequented by shop girls.

I think he took a pleasure in showing me round. I was so easily gratified. He introduced me to his friends. He had once seen me reading a book of poems and this seemed to impress him. He asked me to carry the book about with me so that I could read a poem to some specially selected acquaintances. The result was not always a success. The listener would fidget and look away, or even interrupt, saying perhaps to Stacey: 'I say, Stacey, you remember that——' But Stacey brooked no interference.

'Don't you know it's rude to interrupt. Don't you appreciate good stuff when you hear it?' he would say, raising his gloved hand to command silence.

CHAPTER XX

ENGLISH SUNDAY

A LARGE town on Sunday has a devitalized appearance. The shuttered shops, the empty streets, the absence of normal activity produce in the mind a feeling of negation.

At home I had not experienced this feeling. There the Sabbath quietude had seemed less artificial; it was the natural silence of the fields and meadows which so closely surrounded us; the tranquillity of the country-side took possession of our small town as a matter of course.

On Sunday mornings my father and I sometimes sat or walked in the garden, but usually we attended service at the parish church with my mother. The solemnity of a ritual which I was not old enough to understand oppressed my spirits and I looked forward to the moment when the service would be over. I disliked wearing my best clothes, I felt stiff and unnatural in them. They were associated in my mind with the smell of leather-covered prayer books, dusty hassocks, and the scent of lavender water. When we came out of church, people greeted each other cheerfully as though they were conscious of a sense of relief.

On Sunday evenings my mother would sit at the piano and sing a hymn softly to herself with my father joining in occasionally, or humming the tune when he was not sure of the words. Some perverse puritanical instinct in me opposed any demonstration of sentiment, but I enjoyed listening to my parents and even attempted at times a croaking accompaniment.

Now that I was in a strange town I decided to

experiment by visiting a nonconformist church. I
chose the nearest, which was situated in the main
street almost opposite my place of business. The
first sermon I heard there was a remarkable one. The
preacher spoke of the sin of pride. He told the story
of a plant that grew in a window-box outside a modern
flat. Every evening the plant was watered and a
weed that grew alongside the plant received the
benefit of this watering. The preacher imagined the
weed saying to itself complacently: 'I am receiving
this dispensation as my due from the master of the
house.' But in actual fact the master was absent and
the watering was being done by a conscientious servant
who wished to keep the plant alive and was not even
aware of the tiny weed's existence. The point of the
parable did not escape me, but the story seemed to
hold implications not intended by the preacher. If
the weed was receiving the water by accident, was not
the plant to a lesser degree in the same position? For
if the servant had not been conscientious, the plant as
well as the weed would have died without the absent
master being aware of the fact, or for all I knew even
caring.

I was not in the habit of thinking for myself and felt
rather pleased with my reasoning. The preacher had
aroused in me the very thing he sought to destroy—
the sin of pride. His sermons were so stimulating
that I continued to listen to them and thus, all unconsciously, he became the servant who watered the
weed.

It was at this church that I met Alan Lansing. He
was a tall, well-built young man, who was known
locally for his athletic prowess. He had a frank, open
expression, pink complexion, blue eyes, and a hearty
handshake. He came to me when the church service

*E

was over and expressed his pleasure at seeing me there. Some weeks later he asked me to read a paper to the young men's Bible class, which met on Sunday afternoons in a room adjoining the church. I was given to understand that the subject need not be a biblical one, but that a subject with a moral would be preferred. I had been reading Plutarch's life of Lycurgus, and so chose as my subject the story of the Spartan state. I do not remember introducing a moral to my remarks, but I rather fancy I stressed the idea of social responsibility and co-operation.

This was my first attempt at public speaking and the weight of my responsibility hung heavily upon me. Nightly I laboured to get Plutarch down on paper in a form which I hoped would satisfy the class. I also practised oratory with Stacey as my enthusiastic audience.

When the day for my performance arrived I found about a dozen young men sitting in stolid array in the meeting room awaiting my 'message.' The leader of the class took the chair and introduced me as 'our young friend who has burnt the midnight oil in the pursuit of learning and enlightenment.' I felt highly tensed and almost light-headed with nervousness. My head seemed to swell up like a balloon which threatened to pull me off my feet. When the chairman mentioned 'midnight oil' I had the greatest difficulty in repressing a desire to giggle, because it reminded me of a question put to me one day by Mr. Morgan of the dress department who asked: 'How do you burn a candle at both ends?'

I got to my feet and began to read my paper. I found that my hand was shaking, so to keep the paper still I supported my elbow with my left hand. This was not entirely successful, because I had constantly to remove my supporting hand in order to turn the pages of my manuscript. Every now and then I would remember what I thought to be a striking phrase and this I spoke extempore, but when I had completed my sentence I realized that I had lost my place. To cover up my lapse I quoted other phrases, which I had learnt by heart, only to be disconcerted when upon recovering my place in the manuscript I discovered those same remarks staring up at me from the written page. In a sort of daze I blundered on to the end and sat down with almost an audible sigh of relief.

The chairman thanked me for my interesting paper which, he remarked, 'has given us all much food for thought.' While I had been speaking my eyes seemed to lose the power to focus clearly, but now that I was reseated normal sight was restored to me, and I could see the young men who comprised my audience. They looked exactly the same as when I first entered the room. They sat confronting me with faces entirely devoid of expression.

The Lansings had invited me to their home for tea, so when the Bible class was over Alan and I took the tram to their house. The interior of the house was cool, clean, and airy. A vase of flowers stood on a low table in the hall. The floor was waxed and shining. It was slippery. Every time I lifted my foot I was afraid to put it down again and when it was down I was doubtful about raising it. The hall and corridor were panelled in light oak. There were many windows and the sun seemed to shine in at every one of them. I thought everything about the house modern and wonderful, but I missed the twists and turns, the unexpected bulges and rambling inconsequence of Cornhill House.

The Lansings were very kind to me. They overlooked my gaucherie and did their formal best to make me at home. Mr. Lansing took me out into the garden and showed me the bright smooth-faced lawn, the flowers which seemed to have a special sheen as though they had just washed their faces, and the rambler roses that even in their rambling never lost their sense of direction and decorousness.

We had tea and ate small triangular sandwiches and tiny triangular cakes. During a pause in the conversation I asked if Alan might come to the pictures with me next week. Mrs. Lansing smiled and said it was very kind of me, and I knew I had said something wrong. The conversation turned to tennis and I did my best to discuss the game without betraying the fact that I had never played it. I did not deceive myself that I was successful in my efforts to dissemble and I am certain I did not deceive the Lansings. But the atmosphere of polite conversation persisted; it seemed to entangle and yet sustain our spoken words like a gossamer web——strong, but invisible.

After tea Alan took me upstairs to show me his 'den.' The word den was associated, in my mind, with stories I had read of elderly gentlemen who retired to an airless study that reeked of stale cigar smoke. Alan's den had no relationship to its fictitious counterpart. The windows were open to their fullest extent. The house stood on an elevation and a breeze was scampering round the room. Curtains billowed, pictures danced——everything seemed to be in motion except the leather punch-ball, the Indian clubs, and the dumb-bells, which stood neatly arranged along one side of the room.

Alan lovingly fingered these instruments of physical culture (which to me looked more like instruments of physical torture) and while he did so gave me a detailed account of various exercises which he claimed would develop my chest measurement, strengthen my muscles, and harden my abdominal wall. With the eye of faith I saw myself acquiring physical perfection until I came to look like one of those Herculean figures depicted on the covers of health magazines—all muscle and magnetism. But when I tested the hardness of the punch-ball and the weight of the clubs and dumb-bells, the vision faded and by contrast I felt that I was now even less strong than before I first entered the room.

When it was time for me to go Mr. and Mrs. Lansing gravely shook me by the hand and asked me to come again. But shortly after this visit Alan left home to take up an appointment in London and I did not see him again. The preacher whose sermons had aroused my interest also left the town. My link with the church was broken and it was not long before I ceased to attend the services there.

CHAPTER XXI

A TRIP TO LONDON

Up to the time of my apprenticeship I had maintained a desultory correspondence with Eleanor Carlton. Every year at Christmas we sent each other a book. My gift was usually a copy of some recognized classic or a collection of poems bound in padded leatherette covers, plentifully splashed with gilt decoration.

Except for this annual greeting our letters were few and far between, and then one day I received word from her that she was married and living in London. She gave me her address, a number in Blandford Square.

'We are short of furniture,' she wrote, 'but full of ideas. Do look us up some time.'

About six months later, during the month of October, my employer suggested that I might profit by attending a lecture on salesmanship to be given in London at a trade exhibition. He intimated that, if I wished, I could stay overnight and return to business in the morning. I accepted his offer and booked a room at the small private hotel in Craven Street where I had stayed on a previous occasion.

The lecture began at 5.30 p.m. The speaker, who was an 'efficiency expert,' wore heavy tortoiseshell glasses of the kind favoured by big business executives and which undoubtedly helped to give an imposing appearance to a face which otherwise might be deemed mediocre and commonplace.

The lecture followed the familiar course of elaborating the obvious. The salesman must be polite, attentive, arresting. He must have that psychological insight which would enable him to discern the customer's requirements even before the customer herself had formulated them. If she had a difficulty in making up her mind the salesman must make it up for her.

I felt scornful of these glib commercial platitudes and left the meeting feeling rather pleased with myself. For contempt has the effect of putting us in a superior frame of mind, but if I had known how the evening was to end I might have felt less complacent.

It was now 6.30. Darkness had fallen, but the night was fine and clear. I began to consider how I should spend my time. Then I remembered Eleanor and on the spur of the moment decided to make her a surprise visit. I walked to the nearest underground station and told the booking clerk that I wanted to get to Blandford Square. He gave me a ticket for Marylebone. From here Blandford Square was only a few steps—and I found the house quite easily. There was a light in the front-room window and I thought I heard the sound of voices. I ascended some steps and tugged at the heavy bell knob. It came away three or four inches from the wall and I could hear the bell wires clanking and jangling in the passage on the other side of the door.

As I waited I had a moment of panic because I could not recall Eleanor's married name, but as the door opened it came to me and I said, addressing the dark form confronting me: 'Is Mrs. Hillman in?'

A masculine voice replied: 'Yes, I am Mr. Hillman.'

'Oh,' I said, 'my name is Norman, Norman Hancock.'

I began to apologize for my unannounced call, but Mr. Hillman cut me short, saying in the friendliest manner: 'Of course. Come in. Ellen will be glad to see you.'

The passage was dark. A small gas-jet somewhere

ahead made a wheezy, asthmatic sound, but contributed little illumination. Mr. Hillman took my arm and guided me forward.

'We have a few friends with us,' he said, 'I hope you don't mind.'

This information unnerved me, but I said: 'Oh, no, of course not.'

I followed Mr. Hillman into a room and stood blinking in the strong light. Two men and three women were seated round a coal fire on seats ranging from an oak stool to deck-chairs.

'Ellen,' said Mr. Hillman, 'look whom I 've found on our doorstep.'

Eleanor came forward, saying: 'Why, Norman, this is pleasant.' She put me in an Oxford chair, so low that when I sat down the room and the figures of the seated people seemed to tilt towards me. Eleanor had changed very little since I had last seen her at the school sports nearly four years ago. She had the same air of cool whimsical detachment—and this atmosphere of tranquillity had the salutary effect of putting me at my ease. She introduced me to the company and conversation was resumed, though for the most part I sat silent.

There was an open bookcase immediately beside my chair and under cover of the talk I took stock of the books. Many of the titles were unfamiliar to me, though I recognized some novels of Gissing. There were books of poetry by Yeats and Bridges and a copy of John Masefield's *Nan* in paper covers. Four fat brown volumes entitled *John Christopher* by Romain Rolland stood between some novels by George Moore. Alongside these were *Old Mole* by Gilbert Cannan and plays by J. M. Synge. Mr. Hillman, noticing my interest, came over and invited me to browse through the books.

'Do you know this man?' he said, pulling out a stubby blue-covered book called *The White Peacock*. 'This is his first book so far. Ellen and I rather enjoyed it.'

'No,' I said, looking at the author's name, D. H. Lawrence. 'I'm afraid I am rather ignorant about books.'

'But you like reading?'

'Oh, yes,' I replied, wishing I could say something that was not flat and banal. I opened *The White Peacock* and inside, in small, clear writing, was the inscription: 'Ellen from Richard.'

I felt a pang of jealousy, but it was only a fleeting sensation like the jumping of a nerve. I looked up and saw Mr. Hillman smiling down at me.

'Yes, that's my name,' he said. For no apparent reason we both laughed, and as I looked at his rather heavy expressive features, I knew that I liked him.

Ellen went out to the kitchen to make coffee and sandwiches.

'Come on, Norman,' she said, 'you can give me a hand.'

The kitchen was a vast gloomy place with a large, unused cooking range, a small gas-stove, and very little else. Eleanor asked me all about myself—where was I living, what was I doing?

'I am glad you came,' she said; 'it was nice of you to walk in without any fuss. Do you like Dick's books? They are mostly second-hand. He rummages round the stalls off the Edgware Road when he gets the chance.'

We rejoined the others and, over the sandwiches and coffee, I talked with one of the men about shops and advertising. He was a commercial artist enthusiastic about the future of advertising. This led to a general discussion on the respective merits of large and small businesses, and I caused some amusement by describing the lecture by the 'efficiency expert.'

At length one of the women said she really must go. I was surprised at the lateness of the hour; it was almost eleven o'clock.   I thought I had better leave too, but I felt no sense of urgency.   Never very practical at the best of times, I was inclined to be quite unrealistic under the stimulus of excitement.

'Ann lives at Notting Hill Gate,' said Richard, referring to the girl who was leaving, 'but I suppose you will be going in the opposite direction?'

'Yes,' I replied, 'but I will walk with her to Baker Street station.'

I said good-bye to Eleanor and the others and set off with Ann.

Outside the air was crisp and clear.   One part of me felt light and exalted, the other heavy and tired. The heavy part of me said, Don't be a fool, but the exalted element prompted me to be chivalrous and quixotic.   The nearer we came to the station the more chivalrous I became, until finally I found myself offering to see Ann home.

'Oh, but it's so far out of your way,' she said.

'Not a bit,' I replied, 'won't take me any time to get back.'

We got out at Notting Hill Gate station and walked down two or three streets until we reached a corner house.

'Well, here we are,' said Ann, 'this is where I live.'

The gate made a squealing cry when I pushed it open and a light sprang up behind the fanlight of the house.   The door opened and a female voice said: 'Oh, Ann, I've been waiting up all hours.   Where have you been?'

Ann said over her shoulder to me: 'Thank you so much for coming home with me,' and then she was gone.

The street seemed very quiet now that I was alone. The flat, empty stillness subdued my effervescent mood, leaving me tired and dejected. I walked back to the tube station and arrived on the platform just as a train was coming in. An official shouted: 'Hurry up, there—last train.' I ducked between the closing doors, sat down, relaxed, and in a few moments was asleep.

When I awoke I was sitting in darkness except for a faint gleam of light from somewhere outside the coach. The silence was so intense that it was almost like a physical impact. I peered about me to see what the other passengers were doing, but except for myself the carriage was empty. I thought I was suffering from some sort of hallucination, or perhaps I was not properly awake.

I got to my feet and stamped up and down the coach. But this physical action made not the slightest difference. The lights remained out, the train was motionless, the silence oppressive. I had the feeling of being buried and forgotten. I thought of the tons and tons of earth above me pressing down upon the stillness of the tunnel.

I banged on the window, but even sound seemed subdued and inarticulate. With my face close to the glass I could see a stream of light somewhere round a curve of the tunnel. I wrenched open the sliding doors and stuck my head out. About a hundred yards away, shaped like a half-moon and looking curiously like a stage set, was a brilliantly lit station. I realized then what had happened. The train had been shunted into a siding for the night and I had slept through the whole business. I looked again at the station to see if I could discern any signs of life, but saw only curving walls, posters, entrances, and exits, and the round face of a clock. A clock! I took out my gun-metal watch and found that it had stopped.   I usually wound it up each night at eleven o'clock.   At eleven o'clock I had left Blandford Square.   That seemed hours ago.   I guessed the time must be about one o'clock, perhaps later.   I banged on the window and shouted through the open door.   The station stood dumbly bright—a curved slice of light with dark entrances dotted here and there like black teeth in a fixed grin.

Should I get out and walk along the track?   But there was a double track and I had to reckon with the danger of live rails.   Or did they cut off the current in the early hours?   On the other side of the coach the tunnel wall was only a few inches away, so there was no chance of getting out that way.   I was just about to make myself as comfortable as possible on the seat when I heard the sound of voices.   I looked round the door and saw dark forms bobbing up and down, moving towards the coach from the opposite direction to the station.   I shouted.   Three workmen came into view, halted, and looked at me curiously.   I felt a fool explaining my predicament, but they took it all as a matter of course and guided me to the station platform. There they left me and I climbed the stairs and emerged into the street.   There was no one about, so I walked straight ahead until I came to a crossing.   I stood irresolute looking at the lines of lighted lamp-posts that marched off in four directions.   My eye caught sight of a dark figure standing motionless in a doorway. A policeman. I walked across to him and said:

'Can you tell me if I'm on the right road for Charing Cross?'

'You are out a bit late,' he said, remaining perfectly immobile except for the motion of his lips and the rise and fall of his chin-strap.

'Yes,' I said, extemporizing, 'I lost the last train back to my hotel.'

'Know where you are now?'

'No,' I said.

'Cromwell Road. Keep straight on.'

I was no wiser for the sphinx-like policeman's information, but I set off briskly, overtaking one by one the marching lamp-posts which extended across the metropolis in an endless chain.

I no longer felt tired, only rather lonely and a little fearful of this strange, empty, lunar London. I passed the South Kensington Museum and entered Brompton Road. There was no traffic—though once I heard the whine of a taxi in some distant square—only mile upon mile of lamp-strung streets, empty and shining. The chill, impersonal illumination supplied by hundreds of incandescent globes gave to the radiating avenues of brick, glass, and stone an air of Utopian unreality. Walls stood bleached and cold as skeletons, windows glinted like glass eyes, and the deserted traffic islands seemed to shrink beneath the circumfused light. I thought that if I shouted the brittle air would vibrate, the houses rock, and a thousand ghostly voices answer in echoing reply.

I passed through Knightsbridge and saw the trees of Hyde Park hushed and motionless, their leaves glinting under the artificial light like green eyes. Hyde Park Corner, Green Park, Piccadilly. More petrified policemen now—blue ninepins irregularly spaced. All silent. Only the click of my heels and the wax and wane of my shadow to keep me company.

Piccadilly Circus, Haymarket, the dark finger of Nelson's Column, the narrow black canyon of Craven Street . . . I was standing outside my hotel, my eyes were closing in sleep. Why had I come here? Surely I knew the place would be closed.

I sat down on the steps only to jump up again at the sound of a voice. From an opposite doorway a blue ninepin had come to life.

'Anything wrong?'

I mumbled my story and said: 'Where can I sleep?'

'Well, there's a lodging house just off the Charing Cross Road.'

'Thank you,' I said, and the policeman went back into his trance.

I retraced my steps to the pale emptiness of Trafalgar Square, walked past St. Martin's in the Fields into Charing Cross Road.

The entrance to the doss house was small and narrow. Through the open doorway came a faint gleam of light, and a strong smell of disinfectant. I walked down a passage to the foot of some stairs. A tiny oil lamp burnt on a shelf. To my right a wooden shutter shot up and a face said: 'Fourpence, blanket frippence.'

'What?' I said, only half awake.

'What's the matter wiv yer blasted ears?' said the face, which grew larger until it filled the aperture. 'Do you want a blanket?'

'Yes,' I said.

'Very well then. Fourpence and frippence is sevenpence. A tanner and a blackie, got it?'

I fumbled in my pocket and produced a shilling. 'Keep the change,' I said.

'Thank you, sir. I can see you're all in. Now here you are. A real nice blanket this one. Wivout himpediment or itch. Ha, ha!' He thrust a grey mass of coarse material at me through the hole and the shutter clattered down.

I walked down the stairs and an indescribable stench rushed up at me and smacked me in the face.

I stumbled between rows of prostrate bodies. Open mouths, black and shapeless in the semi-darkness, emitted grunts, sighs, and groans. I found a vacant space, fell down on my blanket, and was asleep.

CHAPTER XXII

OUT OF THE FRYING-PAN

At the conclusion of my two years' apprenticeship I was retained for another year as an 'improver.' Towards the end of this year I began to look around for another berth, or to put it into trade slang, a new 'crib.' I bought a copy of the *Christian Herald*, which was the recognized medium for advertising jobs in the drapery trade, and scanned the small ads. There was certainly a large field—column after column contained appeals for window-dressers, milliners, workroom hands, stock-keepers, buyers, book-keepers, cashiers, assistants, improvers, and apprentices. I pencilled a ring round two of the advertisements—one from north London and the other from the south. The north London advertisement contented itself with a bald assertion, 'Junior Assistant required for the household linens,' the other was more explicit and demanded someone 'young, capable, energetic, and of smart appearance to assist in the Dress and Curtain Departments.' I read this advertisement through several times and came to the conclusion that, of the various qualifications enumerated, the only one that I could honestly lay claim to was the first. However, I decided to apply for the post, and accordingly sat down one evening at the sitting-room table to compose a letter. I had no experience in the writing of business letters, but Mr. Morgan, who was present, volunteered to help me.

'Make out a rough copy first,' he advised, 'and state age, height, and experience. Make it as concise as possible and don't give any unnecessary details.'

'Shall I enclose a photograph of myself?' I inquired.

'No,' said Mr. Morgan. 'Photos are tricky things and you never know how they will strike an employer. He either dislikes what he sees or if impressed fears that the photo may flatter you. The most satisfactory arrangement is to ask for an interview. You will see what sort of a place you are going to and he will have some idea of what he is going to get.'

After a good deal of cogitation I completed my letter and enclosed a self-addressed stamped envelope. Two days later I received a reply asking me to call. I obtained a day off and travelled to Waterloo. From there I took bus and tram to my destination.

The gentleman who interviewed me stared searchingly into my face through gold-rimmed spectacles. I managed to maintain a reasonably calm demeanour and answered his questions in what I hoped was a brisk and business-like manner.

'Well, I think you will do,' he finally concluded. He gave me a smile and relaxed in his chair. 'How's your father?' he inquired.

'Very well, thank you, sir,' I replied. His sudden change of manner, and the fact that he knew my father, threw me off balance and I found it difficult to maintain the conversation. But eventually the interview was terminated and when I left my spirits rose. I had got the job and twenty pounds a year rise.

I found my new job strenuous and exacting. There were no lazy interludes such as I had enjoyed with Stacey—interludes during which we left the shop for the privacy of the cellar, ostensibly to tidy up, but actually to gossip or indulge in day-dreams and mental speculation.

The keynote of the London shop was industry and efficiency. The atmosphere seemed curiously brittle and unreal, like the atmosphere evoked by a Victorian print which idealistically illustrates the background and activities of the model apprentice.

The dress department, which incorporated the curtain and window net section, occupied nearly half the shop. It was staffed by the buyer, a brisk, purposeful man, entirely engrossed in the ethics and practice of business; his lieutenant and 'first sales,' who modelled himself upon his superior; a young man named Ackroyd, and myself.

Ackroyd was also a newcomer. He was tall, thick-set, and rather clumsy in his movements. He had the countryman's slow-moving mind and was not always able to grasp quickly the many instructions that were rapidly fired at him. His heavy, phlegmatic manner aroused irritation and he was often blamed for mistakes which were not of his making, simply because the nature of the mistake seemed to fit him. He welcomed me as an ally—both of us were confused by the current of bustling enterprise and forceful endeavour in which we found ourselves. Caught in the whirlpool of unaccustomed activities we swirled, eddied, and floundered like fish in a mill race, but by joint collective effort we usually managed to get through the day's work without serious mishap.

The terror of the establishment was the telephone. When it rang every member of the staff became pre-occupied with some important task, their faces turned in any direction except towards the black cavity under the staircase where the instrument was situated. Then the buyer's voice would be heard calling imperiously: 'Hancock! Ackroyd! Answer the phone,' and one of us would reluctantly disappear round the corner of the cash-desk into the dark telephone closet, there to grope for the receiver and strain our hearing to distinguish above the noise of the shop the other noise which came to us over the telephone wires. I say 'noise' because it was my experience that women customers usually shouted with their lips close to the mouthpiece, so that on the receiving end the telephone appeared to bark like a dog. Presently, because she was growing tired, or in rare instances because I had advised a less intimate vocal attachment to the mouthpiece, the customer's voice grew more subdued, but as though to make up for lack of volume the words were now spoken with greater speed until they poured into my over-receptive ear like a gushing verbal cascade.

'Saw it in the window last Tuesday, in the morning I think, a pale blue . . . what? oh, yes, a blouse, six and eleven or was it eleven and six, in any case you will know the one it was, on the left-hand side, a pale blue, but have you the same in salmon-pink . . . what do you say, no, not women's—outsize. Can you send it and when may I expect it? Can you hear me? Don't you know what colours you 've got? Not in the size? Well, what sizes and colours have you? Oh, yes, it had short sleeves and I should like it in long sleeves.'

There was a note-pad on a shelf under the telephone. These inquiries and instructions had to be written down in almost total darkness and, from experience, I knew that when I emerged into the light of the shop my writing would be indecipherable. I gave up the idea of trying to write the message and endeavoured to memorize it; but so frequently did the customer chop and change, and so circuitous was her wordy journey, that by the time I had memorized her last utterances I had forgotten the beginning of her remarks, and though firmly convinced that she wanted a blouse I had but the vaguest idea as to price, colour, and size.

A minor terror was a sweet old lady, slightly deaf,

who regularly came into the shop for patterns of dress material. As soon as she was seen to approach, the buyer would whisper fiercely to me: 'Now remember, Hancock, not right across the material, we can't afford it.'

When I displayed the material, the old lady invariably said: 'Will you please cut a piece right across so that I shall have an idea of the width?'

'I am sorry, madam, we are not permitted to cut a piece right across.'

'What's that you say?'

'I am sorry, madam.'

'Oh, dear, young man; don't keep saying you are sorry, you sound so pitiful.' And the old lady would give me a look out of the corner of her eye—a look at once sly and amused—which caused me to reflect that she was not perhaps so deaf as she pretended.

Another minor terror was a younger lady who was always wanting to change things after she had made a purchase.

'I am sorry, but this piece of stuff—it's just two and a half yards—you remember, you served me with it. Well, I think the pattern is a little too large. If you would change it for something with a spot or a small sprig or something . . .'

'Well, madam——'

'Oh, it's quite clean—just as I bought it.'

'Yes, madam; but you see we shall have to sell it now as a remnant and that means a reduction in price.'

'Oh, dear. Fancy that now. What an intricate thing business is!'

My reading at this time was chiefly devoted to books by contemporary authors such as Wells, Galsworthy, and Shaw. These writers appealed to me because they made exciting ideas then current—ideas which had spilled over into the newspapers and magazines, and even into day-to-day conversation.

Wells presented me with a nodding acquaintance with science, a subject which he made glamorous and romantic; Galsworthy appealed to my sentimentality; and Shaw gave me mental stimulation.

But of the arts—painting, sculpture, and music—I had little or no knowledge; while literature—that is to say literature with a big L—meant to me only important names which one saw on the backs of little-used books, handsomely bound and left reverently in peace on the highest or lowest shelves of the public library.

In the assistants' sitting-room, above the shop, I found an illustrated book on G. F. Watts, the Victorian painter, by G. K. Chesterton. I had never even heard of Watts and the pictures were just pictures to me. Ought I to admire them? I did not know. I thought them dull, but perhaps I ought to like them.

I read the book slowly and painfully. I tried to swallow the long sentences, but they stuck in my throat like lengths of spaghetti, half in and half out. Chesterton's aphorisms and paradoxes dazzled and bewildered me. It was like looking at a set piece in a firework display, which has for its chief attraction the portrait of some well-known person. In Chesterton's book the portrait was there, but behind the leaping rockets and wavering lights of the author's paradoxical style it flickered into obscurity.

One day I came across a copy of the *New Age*, the weekly periodical so brilliantly edited by A. R. Orage. Its contents opened up for me totally unexpected vistas, avenues of thought which hitherto had been utterly beyond my conception. The idea of National Guilds, as advocated by Orage, seemed to me at the time the perfect half-way house between the hovels of reaction and the dream-supported mansions of the political idealist.

When Orage's book, *National Guilds*, was published I eagerly secured a copy, but while I was able to grasp, though imperfectly, the general scheme, there were many words in the book unfamiliar to me. I therefore bought a pocket dictionary and during the reading of this *magnum opus* of the Guild Socialist movement, Ackroyd became my assistant and looked up for me the many words which were outside my limited vocabulary.

Engaged in this curious recreation we spent many hours together in the open in parks and on commons, but usually after half an hour of furious concentration we succumbed to the delights of our surroundings. We put the books away and lay full length upon the spiky grass that pushed against the back of the neck like tough, coarse, probing hairs, and half closed our eyes against the sun's seeping heat; or looked at the trees beneath which the sunlight fell in dancing patterns upon the dry, pine-needled earth.

It was not long before I came to the conclusion that I was a misfit and quite useless as a shop assistant. How then was I to become a draper? I could not answer that. I lost heart and performed my duties perfunctorily, treading the days like the treads of a treadmill one behind the other, round and round and round, not without hope for I was buoyant with youth, but with ever-increasing boredom.

And out of doors the summer of 1914 blazed with beautiful indifference. I grew very weary of that long, shining, sun-filled summer. I questioned myself continually as to my future, but was too uncertain and fearful to take any particular action.

On 28th June Archduke Ferdinand of Austria was

murdered in the streets of Sarajevo. This item of news meant very little to me. I was occupied with the trivial affairs of my own small self-enclosed world. A month later Austria declared war against Serbia.

In England the summer holidays had commenced, and towards the end of July the staff of our business spent their annual half-day's outing on the Thames. There was no break in the summer weather and when we climbed aboard the river steamer the sky was cloudless. The head buyer and myself were in charge of the arrangements and I felt important and consequential supervising the seating accommodation and sorting out the sandwiches and cakes in the small cabin below deck. I was wearing my new flannel suit which had cost me forty-five shillings and sported a rose in the buttonhole of my lapel. On the tiny bridge of the boat the 'governor' stood beside the captain. His gold-rimmed spectacles glinted in the sun; he looked carefree and benevolent, but his alert eyes darted about behind his glasses in their customary business-like manner.

The boat chug-chugged up the river until we reached an island, where we disembarked for a picnic tea. Returning home in the dark we sang sentimental songs and someone played an accordion. One of the bolder spirits wanted to sing *Alexander's Ragtime Band*, but was persuaded to abandon the idea in case the governor should object. In revenge he sang Tosti's *Good-bye* very plaintively. The words 'Good-bye to summer, good-bye, good-bye,' seemed to move him almost to the point of tears.

The next day, 31st July, we resumed our normal duties behind the counter and on that same day Germany dispatched an ultimatum to Russia.

By midnight, 4th August, England and Germany were at war.

At first the war was not taken very seriously; it would be over by Christmas. There were thousands of volunteers for the army and later the white feather brigade got to work, but whether one did or did not join up was a matter of conscience. The slogan 'Business as Usual' gave indirect support to those who felt they could not be spared from essential services. A cousin of mine, who in any case was over military age, was asked if he would like to be a soldier. He replied, enigmatically: 'I prefer walking.' This might be compared with the reply of the painter Cézanne who, when asked, 'What did you do in the war [of 1870]?' explained: 'I was working on a design.'

CHAPTER XXIII

MARS IN THE ASCENDANT

AT the end of August I returned home for my annual fortnight's holiday. Everything there seemed much the same. The old horse-drawn bus met me at the station. The same driver who had once given me a 'whip-behind' now greeted me with a broad smile.

'Any luggage, Mr. Norman?' he inquired.

'No, Joe, just the suitcase.'

We trundled off down the long hill that led to the town; to the left I could see the square, ivy-covered tower of the church, and beyond on higher ground the brown stone buildings of the grammar school.

Soon we were in the main street, mildly alive with its small, intimate activities. The market square was almost deserted and as the bus rounded the town hall I saw my father come out of the shop door to help an apprentice unpack a crate of millinery that leaned drunkenly against the pavement's edge.

My mother had prepared an early tea and we had the dining-room to ourselves. Our voices seemed loud and strong in this quiet place. Occasional sounds, the banging of the shop door, the cook clattering pans and dishes in the kitchen, a bird chirruping under the eaves of the roof came to me out of the surrounding silence with unconfused clarity.

After tea I wandered through the rooms and corridors of Cornhill House seeing familiar things in new and unaccustomed perspective. The negro statuettes with the scimitars were in their usual place above the main staircase. They looked smaller and less aggressive now. I thought it strange that these innocent ornaments had once frightened me, and half hoping to recapture the old flesh-creeping thrill I pushed open the door of the lumber-room and entered the once-dreaded Bluebeard's chamber. The female dummies were still there, but one of the waxen heads had fallen from the dusty shelf and lay on the floor, its face upturned in an inane smile. I picked it up and replaced it beside a broken wooden horse. The ginger-coloured mane of the horse had come unstuck and hung limply across its black boot-button eyes. The room had lost its atmosphere of fearful expectancy; it was just a dirty, neglected rubbish hole. Downstairs the assistants were leaving their sitting-room on their way to bed. I passed them on the stairs and said good night. I knew none of them; they were all strangers. Even Mr. Tomkins of the gents' outfits had left some years since.

I looked in the assistants' sitting-room. The gas was out, but I relit the burner with a match from a box on the mantelshelf. Directly alongside the gas bracket was a notice in my father's familiar and characteristic handwriting.

NOTICE

If you leave the room empty turn the gas down. If you are the last one going to bed *turn the gas right out*.

Assistants must leave this room by 10.10 every night.

Assist in keeping the room tidy—do not strike matches on the wall, or stick needles in the paper.

Let the servant know on Wednesdays at 1 o'clock if in to tea.

Also let her know by Saturday night if you will

F

be in to DINNER *or* TEA on Sunday—it will then be laid.

Careful not to jar the GAS MANTLE.

I put out the light.
The European war seemed very far away.

But the war was nearer than I realized, and neither the homespun tranquillity of Cornhill House nor the smiling face of the surrounding countryside could prevent its sombre intrusion. It was a flaming banner on the front pages of the newspapers, a nagging question mark at the back of every man's mind. Daily we read of the German advance through Belgium and across France, until the grey armies were but a few miles from the outskirts of Paris.

'Things look grave,' said my father one morning at breakfast, and this simple statement did more to bring the position home to me than all the newspaper reports, for my father had to a marked degree the British habit of understatement.

On the evening of that day a recruiting meeting was held in the town hall. My father, who was a member of the urban district council, attended in an official capacity and my mother and I accompanied him. The assembly room, sunless and chilly, smelt of dust and pitch-pine. In the centre of the platform was a table draped with a large Union Jack, behind which were grouped various notables of the district, including a general in uniform who was to make the chief speech of the evening. He was an earnest but not very inspiring speaker and during the course of his remarks my thoughts wandered. The meeting had for me a dreamlike quality. The rows of quiet respectable people and the monotonous clipped voice of the speaker seemed to have no connection with the titanic struggle that was being waged on the other side of the Channel.

When I thought of war my mind conjured up pictures I had seen in old copies of the *Illustrated London News*, illustrations to stories of heroism; a soldier standing beside a wounded comrade firing over the body of a dying horse, the sky above him full of exploding shells that looked like blobs of splashed ink.

Odd lines, phrases, and fragments of verse passed through my mind. 'The British square,' 'The thin red line,' 'Up, Guards, and at 'em,' 'Into the valley of Death rode the six hundred.'

Inconsequently I thought of the brilliant ball on the eve of Waterloo, and the burial of Sir John Moore. The line, 'Not a drum was heard, not a funeral note,' swam across my mental vision. I recalled the rollicking verse of Kipling, and the words of the popular song:

> Good-bye, Dolly, I must leave you
> For the front to fight the foe.

Such were my hazy, romantic, and entirely unrealistic notions of one of the greatest of all realities.

The general concluded his address with an appeal for recruits and about a dozen men tramped up to the platform from the rear of the hall. For the most part they were agricultural labourers, many of whom had come straight from the fields dressed in their workaday clothes. They shuffled up the steps that gave access to the platform and stood bunched together, their faces wooden and expressionless or creased into sheepish smiles. The audience signified their approval with loud acclamatory hand-clapping, while some of the more excited members shouted words of sympathy and encouragement.

Not even in thought did I associate myself with the active participants in this scene. All my life I had stood in the background, a spectator on the fringe of events. And so on this evening too I remained an onlooker.

After the recruiting meeting the war again receded from my mind. Summer, so early begun, continued to reign with all the serenity of a long-lived monarch. Day followed day, cloudless, burnished with light.

I discovered among my father's books a copy of *Dr. Nicola* by Guy Boothby, which I took into the garden to read. The humming silence of the August afternoon contrasted pleasantly with the esoteric Nicola.

Towards the end of my holiday I spent three days at Seaton with my mother. We put up at an hotel on the front and at night I went to sleep to the sound of the sea. The waves broke upon the beach with soft reverberations. The tiny muffled explosions beat like a pulse upon my ear and even invaded my dreams.

During the day time we crunched about on the big slippery pebbles of the shore, bone-dry and shining under the heat of the sun; or explored the streets of the town and examined the shops, which displayed in their windows a massed assortment of souvenirs, from picture postcards, purses, and shell-encrusted work-boxes to china vases, ashtrays, and cups and saucers— all decorated with lurid views of Seaton.

In the cool of the evening we sometimes walked across the cliffs to Beer and paused awhile to lean over the iron railings on the front and look down on the tiny enclosed bay that seemed made to order to satisfy a nineteenth-century conception of the picturesque.

Thus happily engaged, I imagined I had put the war in its place, or perhaps it would be more accurate to say that I never consciously gave it a thought.

But in the train on my return journey to London, a surprising thing happened. Suddenly, unexpectedly, impulsively, I made up my mind to join the army. The idea came to me without any sort of preliminary warning. It was as though some part of me that I had never known or conjectured had issued a command.

I looked at my fellow passengers and wondered if they were conscious of my excitement. I felt as if I had undergone a physical change that must be immediately apparent to all who saw me.

The more sober part of my mind—like a teasing questioner at a meeting who interjects remarks from the back of the hall—reminded me of prosaic facts.

'Have you forgotten your physical disability?' said the jeering voice. 'You have a hole in your throat, a permanent tracheotomy. Remember?'

But I was impervious to these questioning doubts, and shortly after my return to business I took the first opportunity of putting my resolution to the test. There was no difficulty in finding a recruiting office. From the walls of grey, official-looking buildings the menacing figure of Kitchener pointed with outstretched hand: 'Your King and Country need you.'

After I had been examined the need became less apparent. I was rejected. To my considerable surprise the doctor did not even glance at my throat, but I was told that I was two inches short of the required height.

I tried again in another part of London. This time instead of holding my head down to hide the scar on my throat I extended myself to my full stature.

'Ah,' said the doctor, 'a tracheotomy, that 's not so good. And your chest measurement is not up to standard. Sorry, rejected.'

I now reached the conclusion that Kitchener's army did not want me, so I made a round of the territorial units. I tried to join the City of London Regiment, but they were full up.

A stockbroker who was on the same errand exclaimed: 'Oh, I see, oversubscribed.'

However, I was not yet defeated. I made another attempt and this time was successful.

'Does that scar bother you?' inquired the doctor in tones of the greatest unconcern.

'No, sir,' I replied promptly.

'Good. Passed.'

I pulled on my coat with trembling hands. I was in. I gave my name and particulars to a corporal.

'Home or foreign service?' he asked.

I had not realized that the army would be so considerate as to offer me this alternative and replied almost automatically: 'Foreign.' For this I was given a small badge to wear as a distinguishing mark.

When I told my employer the news he congratulated me. 'Do you know,' he said, 'we have only two men eligible for the services, so now we can claim that fifty per cent of the staff have joined up.'

He generously offered me half pay during my term of service, but asked me if I would stay on with him for another two weeks to give him time to replace me. I went back to the recruiting office with this request, which was immediately granted. The army was certainly very accommodating.

When the members of the staff heard that I had enlisted they showed intense surprise. 'Why did you do it?' they asked, and for the life of me I could not find a reply. Sometimes I asked myself the same question. Not because I had any regrets, but because, when I looked at the matter coldly, I was surprised myself. I came to no conclusion except that it was the result of some powerful, overwhelming impulse, and if you attempt to analyse impulse you may be sure that reason will cook up some sort of answer for the occasion.

Looking back, I think—but with no degree of certainty—that the following factors played their part: desire for self-assertion, love of adventure, boredom with my employment, revolt against my sheltered life, and love of doing the unexpected.

CHAPTER XXIV

CIVILIAN SOLDIER

THE drill hall to which I had been told to report was situated in a quiet residential street. As I was about to enter I was greeted by a small weedy-looking man with a muffler round his neck.

'You joined this lot, mate?' he inquired.

'Yes,' I said.

'Ah, don't let them put nothing over on you. You got to box clever with these army blokes, see.'

I realized he was trying to be friendly and asked him his name.

'Clark,' he replied, giving me a sidelong look from small, heavy-lidded eyes.

'Glad to know you, Nobby,' I said.

He grinned and we shook hands. Inside the hall about thirty men were standing in front of a trestle table. 'Line up with the rest,' said a voice, and Nobby Clark and I took our places behind the others. We shuffled forward in turn. When I came opposite to the N.C.O. behind the table he asked me my name and handed me a slip of paper on which was written a name and address.

'This is your billet,' he said. 'Pack a suitcase or something and move in there to-day.'

He then handed me a typewritten form to which were clipped a number of pink vouchers.

'That form contains a list of restaurants and coffee shops. The attached vouchers to be handed in when you get a meal. Includes breakfast, dinner, and tea. Understand?'

'Yes,' I said. But when I had moved away to make

room for the next man, a number of questions jogged about in my mind. What time must I be in my billet? Could I attend any of the restaurants for a meal? And what was I required to do between meals? As I stood in hesitation I heard the N.C.O. call out:

'Roll-call outside the hut to-morrow morning at nine o'clock. That's all to-day.'

On my way out Nobby Clark caught up with me. 'Well, mate,' he said, 'I'm off home. Gawd, what an army!'

And he departed happily whistling *Cock of the North*.

I came out into the sunshine in some bewilderment. The other men passed me, walking off in various directions, until I was alone. 'You are in the army now,' I said to myself, 'and all you have to do is eat, sleep in a billet, and attend roll-call in the morning. No uniform, no rifle, no drill.' That's all to-day, the N.C.O. had said, so apparently I was free to do as I liked.

Well, that suits me, I thought, yet I felt at a loss. My time was my own and the whole day was before me. I walked along slowly, disconcerted by my freedom. I came to a park and sat down on a seat. People passed me—an errand boy with a parcel under his arm, an old man with a rubber-tipped walking-stick, nursemaids pushing prams. I imagined them looking at me, thinking perhaps that I was out of work.

Presently when I had arranged my thoughts into some sort of order I got up and walked briskly towards my place of business. I decided that my first job was to move my things to my billet and get acquainted with the people of the house.

As I walked along the street of small stucco-fronted houses I glanced at the piece of paper with the address: 'P.C. Jenkins, 43 Park Street.' Thirty-nine, forty-one,

* F

forty-three—there it was, undistinguished from the rest except that the tiny square of grass behind the railings was rather more neat and trim than the neighbouring gardens. I rapped the knocker and a pleasant-faced woman in a print overall opened the door. We stared at each other for a moment, and then she said:

'I expect you are Mr. Hancock. Come in.' She led the way upstairs. 'This is your room. I hope you will be comfortable.'

The room was small, bright, and spotlessly clean.

'If there is anything you want let me know,' said Mrs. Jenkins.

'Thank you,' I said, 'thank you very much.'

'I expect you feel a little strange,' she said.

'Well, yes, I do rather.'

'You will soon get used to it. What are you going to do with yourself all day? Have you got to go back to the drill hall?'

'No,' I said, 'I have some vouchers here to get my meals and then I report again to-morrow morning.'

'Well,' said Mrs. Jenkins, 'I should go out and enjoy yourself. My husband is on duty all day. We have supper at eight-thirty. Suppose you join us then.'

I thanked her and she left me to unpack. I wondered what Mr. Jenkins did for a living. I looked again at the slip of paper with the address. P.C. Jenkins. Why, of course, Mr. Jenkins was a policeman.

I had my dinner at a coffee shop and ordered the 'speciality of the house,' which was 'toad-in-the-hole' (sausage embedded in batter pudding). I spent the afternoon in the park with a book, had an early tea, and then went to a cinema. The commissionaire saw my badge and gave me a free pass. They were showing a French film, by Pathé Frères, about the adventures of a master criminal called Zagomar. He constantly eluded the police by resorting to elaborate disguises. First he was an old man with a long beard, then an aristocratic Englishman with a straw hat and a monocle. Finally he became a hunchback with a patch over one eye. Towards the end of the film he was almost caught by the vigilant gendarmerie, but made his escape in a church where he disappeared through a secret panel in the side of a tomb.

When I came out of the cinema it was eight o'clock, so I made my way back to my billet. Mrs. Jenkins was getting supper ready and P.C. Jenkins was sitting in his shirt-sleeves reading the evening paper. Over supper I recounted the story of my adventures on the night I fell asleep in the tube train, with special reference to the laconic policeman. P.C. Jenkins was highly diverted and roared with laughter.

After supper he showed me his books, for he was a serious reader and enjoyed historical works, such as Gibbon's *Decline and Fall*, and Motley's *Rise of the Dutch Republic*. He told me he never read fiction—in fact despised it. 'What is the use of reading about imaginary people and events,' he said, 'when you can enjoy accounts of real happenings.' I felt there must be an answer to this, but was not able to think of one.

My first week in the army was almost entirely devoted to hanging about in the drill hall. As we were not likely to get uniforms for some time, the army paid us for the wear and tear of our civilian boots, suits, and underclothing. Almost every day we lined up to receive odds and ends of money, sometimes as little as ninepence and sometimes as much as five shillings. Everybody thoroughly enjoyed this procedure, particularly Nobby, who exclaimed: 'Cor stone the crows, it 's money for jam!'

During the second week a very elementary course of training was started. Every afternoon we did a short route march led by a young officer and a veteran sergeant-major. We looked a very unmilitary contingent, but swung along briskly and for the most part in step.

We passed the draper's shop where I had so recently served as an assistant. Incautiously I remarked to Nobby, who was my immediate neighbour in the ranks: 'That 's where I used to work.'

'Wot was you,' said Nobby innocently, 'a porter?'

'Well, no, not exactly,' I replied. 'What were you in civil life, Nobby?'

'Artificial wig restorer,' he said.

I thought it was Nobby's idea of a joke, but later discovered this description on his army papers under the heading 'Previous Employment.'

When the battalion had reached full strength we left London and continued our training under canvas in the Weald of Kent. All about us woods and fields glowed with a serene autumnal beauty. The days passed swiftly. They were bright, still, halcyon days. It was as though the weather was celebrating the end of an epoch before a new and less pleasing period came into being.

Eventually when our training was completed we were drafted to France, there to become a part of the shifting kaleidoscope of war. The surrealistic picture of no man's land replaced the ordered artistry of English fields.

My first winter in France was spent in the waterlogged trenches of Festubert. The weather deteriorated until the contending armies were bogged down in the mud. The heavy guns grew quiescent, their thunder ceased. Smaller engines of artillery became vocal, but at last they too were stilled, and silence covered the tortured, rain-sodden earth.

Then, as though awaiting their moment, the elements laid down an icy barrage upon friend and foe alike. In the words of an old English poet it was for us:

> The thorney wayes, the deep valeis,
> The snow, the frost, the reyn.

The scene of desolation that surrounded us at eye level had a perverse and twisted beauty. In the leaden light of a January afternoon tree stumps were spears of silver, or black daggers upraised at every angle against the sky. A group of brickstacks in the near distance had been pounded by gun fire into pyramidal formations so that they stood in the gathering dusk like obelisks—anonymous monuments to annihilation.

I remember most clearly the moonlit nights when the eerie beauty of no man's land was intensified. Night brought its own individual and particular silence—a silence which the occasional staccato stutter of a solitary machine-gun seemed only to accentuate, as though the sound of the gun was a punctuation mark between long pregnant paragraphs of stillness.

When the moon was high and full it revealed a lutescent world that reminded me of my childhood's oft-recurrent dream. Here was the same stillness, the same sense of immobility and unreality, with the yellow light falling from the sky and the brickstacks transformed by the moon into piles of ochrous rock.

To escape the boredom of the trenches I volunteered for any sort of job that was going. In addition to guarding a mental case in hospital, serving in the cook-house, pumping water from La Bassée Canal, and acting as a brigade runner, I spent three months working underground with Welsh miners in a tunnelling company. Later I rejoined my battalion at Mont St. Éloi where we took over from the Canadians the defence of Vimy Ridge. It was curious to find in the midst of that much-fought-over land the remains of a dug-out used by the French in the war of 1870.

As the result of a shrapnel wound in the foot and a bout of trench fever I joined the long stream of walking wounded on their journey to the base. During convalescence at Étaples the army became for the first time immensely curious about my tracheotomy. R.A.M.C. brass hats gathered round me and plied me with questions. No middle-aged matron eager to discuss her latest operation had a more attentive audience than I had on this occasion. Such sudden and unexpected limelight was embarrassing—I felt like a freak, which no doubt from a medical point of view I was. Finally a medical board concluded this chapter in my army life by marking me category B2, and my days as a fighting soldier were over. From Étaples I was sent to Boulogne where I worked as a clerk in the office of the embarkation medical officer until the end of the war. In February 1919 I was demobilized and presented with a scrap of paper which certified me as being free from lice and scabies. With this evidence of battle upon me I departed for home.

CHAPTER XXV

THE OTHER SIDE OF THE COUNTER

THE discharged soldier, like the traveller home from his wanderings, returns to the country of his origin feeling lost and strange. He looks with unaccustomed eye upon familiar landmarks and discovers in old associations a new world; his mind is without power of accommodation.

In my own case I had security and the interest afforded by new employment. My father had opened a business in a west of England cathedral city, and while Cornhill House was still retained as a branch of the firm it was to the new business that I journeyed to take up my duties as my father's assistant.

And here, after a period of restlessness, I found a new beginning. I was now on the other side of the counter and in addition I liked and respected the people with whom I did business.

As of old, many of our customers were country people and the sight of their comely faces, the sound of their soft drawling voices, pleased and contented me. Though they were often badly dressed and wore colours loud in contrast, yet in some undefinable way their appearance was in keeping with their rugged kindness and rural shrewdness. Fashion is a matter of environment, but harmony has some deeper origin. These humble men and women of field and farmstead possessed a natural courtesy, their simplicity was less tiring than the elusive brilliance of sophistication.

The building in which the new business was conducted was known as 'London House' and dated from the reign of Charles II.   According to tradition a retail drapery business had been carried on there without interruption for three hundred years, from the time when the draper hung a bale of cotton outside the premises to indicate the nature of his trade.

In many respects London House was not unlike Cornhill House.   It too faced a market square; and the rooms above the shop, with their uneven floors, the twisting stairways, winding passages, and deep mysterious recesses, had all the appeal and many of the inconveniences of antiquity.

When some alterations were made to increase the light above one of the darker stairways a parchment document was found, which set out in detail the pay and working hours for apprentices under the trade guilds of the Middle Ages.   To those who think that progress can be likened to a steady upward line, the reasonable conditions set forth in this document would come as a surprise and might lead one to suppose that the graph of human progress corresponds more closely to the medical chart of a fever patient.

When the cattle market was held in the square a large number of people flocked into the town from every point of the compass.   A few arrived by train or by the new motor coaches which had just begun to operate over long distances, but the majority travelled by the older type of horse-drawn carrier's cart—ramshackle contrivances of wood and canvas which trundled along at about five miles an hour.

This welcome army of invaders arrived round about eleven o'clock in the morning and departed at two-thirty or three o'clock in the afternoon.   During that time the shop was thronged with people and our staff snatched a meal at any odd moment during a momentary lull.

There was not much time for detached observation

or reflection, but occasionally I found myself looking out of the doorway at the market scene and the picture I saw reminded me of a Dutch painting. The weather-beaten faces of farmers and drovers, the dumpy figures of cheerful country women, formed a frieze against a background of cattle stalls, farm wagons, and pig pens. Along two sides of the square stood the stalls of market-gardeners, and here also were vendors of crockery, clothing, books, fancy goods, fish, and confectionery.

But soon my attention would be recalled to the immediate business of the shop, the activities of which seemed to be an extension of the larger movement outside. I would hear perhaps an elderly country woman say as she tried on a hat heavily ornamented with the ripest of artificial cherries:

'I don't like thick. 'E be too colourful for I.'

And my glance would be drawn not to the millinery creation upon her head, but to the group of small children clinging to her skirts, their thumbs in their mouths, their eyes fixed upon me in wide and solemn appraisal.

Our assistants were themselves mostly country born and bred; they knew the habits and tastes of their customers. They knew too that the men liked to be chaffed and many a merry jest was exchanged and enjoyed.

There was, for instance, a young farm labourer who shopped for his invalid mother. When he had bought a length of mantel bordering for the fireplace and, perhaps, a brightly coloured chenille table-cloth or a pink marcella quilt for the best bedroom, the woman assistant who served him would be sure to remark:

'Well, Sam, what about a nice handkerchief for your best girl? Don't say you haven't got one. I expect if the truth was known you 're engaged already.'

And Sam, delighted at these personal references, would shift from one foot to the other, a broad grin on his flushed face, and mutter: 'Aw, naow, I ain't got much ter do wi' young ladies.   I 'm kind of shy like.'

Such incidents linger in the memory long after the closing of the shop door.   They clothe the naked skeleton of commercialism in warm human flesh. Looking back I wish that a Rowlandson had been present at those homely encounters to record such scenes in gaily coloured aquatints for the pleasure of posterity.

Shopping in our chromium-plated age has become impersonal.   In the past customers sat up at the counter and took their ease.   To-day they stand or wander in an atmosphere of polite detachment from one vast central-heated department to another.

It was in this setting, among such simple surroundings, that I re-learnt my trade and prepared to take over the administration and management of the business.   There were diversity and interest in the work.   The business had its own customs and methods—customs which had grown up slowly from the past, methods based on experience and the salutary results of trial and error.   Those things could not be taught by rule of thumb and no text-book could hope to indicate the nature of the particular problems involved.   Such problems were part of, and peculiar to, the individual growth of the business.

A son who enters his father's business is expected to make suggestions for improvement.   The subject of 'post orders' reminds me that it is not always wise to interfere with accustomed procedure.   We had a very easy and primitive method of dealing with post orders to the wholesale.   Every day assistants noted down on a piece of paper the immediate needs of their department. This piece of paper, containing the assistant's number for reference, was put on a 'spike.' At the end of the day I collected the order slips, as we called them, and as each order was dealt with I crossed it through, added the date and put it back on the spike with a piece of coloured cardboard on top.

Travellers from stationery firms, who called on us with the latest and most up-to-date examples of duplicate and triplicate order form books, regarded our humble method with scorn. They gently hinted that what was good enough for my father ought not to be good enough for me.

In the end I succumbed to their blandishments and bought a nicely bound decorative-looking book, inter-leaved with carbon paper, which allowed all orders to be entered in triplicate—one for the assistant, one for myself, and one to send to the wholesaler.

But, alas, the goddess of progress proved untrust-worthy. In the first place assistants, using blunt stumpy pencils, bore so heavily upon the thin paper in their efforts to make the carbon perform its job that the paper split and tore. Our wholesalers were not always able to decipher the writing and, worst of all, the book, passed from hand to hand round the shop, was constantly lost or mislaid. In the end we reverted to our original system. The spike once more came into its own. Indeed, it acquired an added status and was enshrined henceforth in our minds as the embodiment of the virtues of simplicity.

The only way to learn to ride a horse is to get on its back. To master the business I had to familiarize myself with all its activities and moods, keep it in its stride, know when to tighten or loosen the rein on expenditure.

In normal times it is easy to overbuy and this results in the tying up of capital which might well be put to better use. On the other hand, it is an equally mistaken policy to underbuy. Nothing creates such a bad impression on a customer as empty or partly filled shelves or lack of assortment.

To steer a straight course between the two extremes is not always easy. The best method is to concentrate on goods in demand for which the business has established a reputation, while leaving a margin for experiment and development.

Sometimes failure can be turned to success by some simple readjustment or even by accident. I once bought a number of flannelette sheets which were priced to sell at 3s. 11d. per pair, but although displayed prominently in the window for several weeks on end only a few pairs sold. I then hit on the idea of selling them singly instead of in pairs. I changed the price tickets and marked them 1s. 11½d. each. In a few days the entire stock was cleared and from that time we sold them in such quantities that I was obliged to place orders with half a dozen wholesalers in order to maintain the supply.

To attempt to buy without a thorough acquaintance with the nature of the goods required is tantamount to putting the cart before the horse and then filling the cart with useless material and finding no possibility of shifting it.

During my apprenticeship I had gained knowledge of two departments only—the 'Manchester' and the 'dresses.' On one occasion I asked my employer's permission to serve in the lace department, but he looked askance at this proposal. Service in the 'laces' was by long tradition an occupation for women only, and although I offered to take a reduction in salary the 'governor' remained adamant in his refusal.

This lack of general experience has in many cases resulted in confusion for the man who sets up in business for himself.

So now I determined to face the temporary embarrassment of handling and serving such articles as women's underclothing, hosiery, and hats. I say temporary embarrassment because habit and use soon put such employment on a neutral basis. Indeed, it was in the buying of millinery and infants' wear that I eventually became most efficient. I liked to experiment. Colour and design appealed to me. These departments were also the most profitable; there are at least two things for which a woman will pay a good price—a new hat for herself and a dainty outfit for her child.

And perhaps this gives a clue to one of the qualities essential to the retail draper, namely, some knowledge, be it conscious or unconscious, of the psychology of the woman purchaser.

One curious effect of buying for other people's needs is the development of a sixth sense—a selling or market sense. In course of time I found myself acquiring an added taste, since the taste of my customers was not always my own personal taste.

A piece of cretonne, for instance, which was a good selling line, might have a colour and design that was personally displeasing. But when I saw it in the wholesale my eye was at once favourably attracted to it because of its commercial value, yet I never found these conflicting values in any way debasing. On the contrary, I began to develop a broader and more tolerant attitude towards taste in general. For once we understand why people like things, whether it be architecture, art, or fashion in clothes, we begin to appreciate tastes other than our own, to respect diversity of appeal, and even to become interested in what we once despised. The good taste of yesterday may become the bad taste of to-day. But who knows whether it will be good or bad taste to-morrow?

During the war I had read few books of any importance. My mind remained a void as far as literature was concerned. Now I began to look about me, hungry for mental stimulation. I discovered the Russian novelists. For the first time I read Tolstoy, whose books hitherto I had seen only on view in back streets in small newspaper shops in which the *Kreutzer Sonata*, with a lurid paper cover depicting a scene of murder, was to be found between the *Police Gazette* and the Sexton Blake Library. After the straightforward realism of Tolstoy the tense, introspective novels of Dostoevsky demanded closer attention and I turned for relief to the humour of Gogol's *Dead Souls*, or to the matter-of-fact style of Maxim Gorky. Gorky in his stories of social realism such as *Twenty-six Men and a Girl* reminded me of the work of Jack London, which perhaps accounts for the popularity of Jack London in Russia.

I also rediscovered on my shelf some copies of *Plays Worth Reading*—paper-covered books published at sevenpence each by Henderson's of Charing Cross Road, then known as the 'Bombshop,' presumably because of the explosive nature of the literature sold there. Among the plays were Anton Chekhov's *Seagull*, Ibsen's *Pillars of Society*, and Strindberg's *Miss Julie*. I probably bought them during my early days in the army, and, finding them rather too strong a meat for my mental digestion, had left them almost unopened. I now read them with absorbed interest.

Another rediscovery was several volumes of the English metaphysical poets, including Donne, Cowley, and George Herbert, which were tucked away behind other books on the shelf of my one solitary bookcase. During my apprenticeship I had attended evening lectures on the seventeenth-century poets and these books contained on any blank space available my painstaking but often inaccurate and badly spelt notes. Here was a feast of magnificent verse indeed in which sensual indulgence, mystical inspiration, and religious fervour were mixed in rich profusion. The lines seemed to leap to my eyes with the brilliance and sparkle of precious stones, and though my mind was now more ready to receive them, yet much of their meaning was still beyond my power of comprehension.

I also, in one solitary instance, tried my hand at economics. The Bolshevik revolution in Russia had created a more general demand for the work of Karl Marx. I attempted to master his *Das Kapital*, but was at last obliged to cry in the words of the psalmist: 'Such knowledge is too wonderful and excellent for me: it is high, I cannot attain unto it.'

I consoled myself with the thought that William Morris has experienced the same difficulty.

EPILOGUE

ONE morning, at the end of August 1922, I sat at a
table with my father in a small room above the shop.
This room, used as an office, was once a sitting-room
and was still known by that name. The most promi-
nent article of furniture was a large roll-top desk.
Beside it in a dark corner stood a safe which my father
had bought at a sale. It was a church safe, many years
old, and had originally been built into a solid wall.
When removed a part of the wall had come away with
it and the iron sides were enclosed in a jagged envelope
of stone. The heavy cumbersome key, six inches in
length, was at the moment wearing a hole in the lining
of my coat pocket.

Round the walls of the room, which were papered
in a pattern of deep red, hung framed photographs of
the shop, each one illustrating an incident in its history.
In one of the pictures the shop front formed a centre
for a number of converging roads and was entitled:
'All roads lead to Hancocks.' Another showed a
scene on opening day. Round the shop door a crowd
of women were struggling for admittance and across
the windows were posters announcing the sale of three
recently purchased stocks. In the foreground a
baby's pram, perched on enormous wheels, was
attended by a small boy who was smiling into the face
of the camera.

The table of the 'sitting-room' was covered with a
length of red art serge, and on this particular day the
only object on the wide expanse of cloth was a legal
document entitled 'Deed of Partnership.'

My father picked it up, adjusted his horn-rimmed
spectacles, turned the crackling pages, and began to

explain to me the nature of some of the more important clauses. There were eighteen altogether, written in bold copper-plate handwriting. On the bottom of the last page a space was left for the signature of the partners.

'Before we sign,' said my father, 'you had better read the whole thing through carefully. In the meantime I have one or two calls to make in the town so I 'll join you later in the shop.'

When I was alone I took up the deed and began to read it. Before turning over the final page I glanced up at the wall in front of me, and there, in the middle of the framed pictures, was a photograph of Cornhill House taken many years ago when my father first took over the business. And immediately my thoughts were diverted, for during the previous week I had paid a visit to my old home for the first time in eight years.

The country station looked like an enlarged model— a footbridge at one end, a signal-box at the other, and in between the low compact building which housed waiting-room, ticket office, and the private quarters of the station master. When the train had disappeared round a bend in the line the small sounds of the place reasserted themselves—the humming of the telegraph wires, the steps of a few passengers on the platform, and the voice of a solitary porter counting aloud a number of parcels. A long way off, somewhere behind the bright sunshine, an alien wind gave an occasional half-hearted moan.

I was the last to leave the platform. I had stopped to look at the penny-in-the-slot machine and to wonder if it was the same eccentric machine that I had known as a child. I could not tell. All station slot-machines look alike—scarred, weather-hardened, they wear a slightly raffish air. I passed through the booking hall with its worn, dusty boards, looked through an open door at the empty waiting-room, and came out into the station yard. The bus that was just about to start was unfamiliar to me. The old horse-drawn vehicle had gone, the new one had more than one horse-power to propel it. A young man who occupied the driving-seat looking inquiringly in my direction, but I shook my head. The motor bus sped on its way leaving me to walk leisurely behind.

I left the station yard with its grass verge and white railings, its stack of coal black against the tiny office of the local coal merchant, and passing the Station Hotel began my journey down the winding road to the town. I arrived at the spot where as a boy I had crouched against the wall to avoid a runaway horse. The wall was no longer there. Trim fences enclosed lawns and gardens behind which villas of red brick stood in detached and upstart pride, but as I looked around me I could see, half hidden by trees on a distant hill, the mellow stones of the grammar school, while below me, and slightly to the left, the tower of the parish church rose squarely above the clustered roofs of the town.

At the beginning of the main street was the news-agent's where once I bought my weekly copy of the *Marvel*. There were many papers tucked into the wire frame hung outside the doorway, but no copy of the *Marvel* was among them. Instead of the thin features of Stanley Dare, the boy detective, I now saw staring at me from the front page of the *Magnet* the round owlish face of Billy Bunter.

I turned off from the main street and made a detour that would take me through the churchyard. On the way I paused before a dwelling upon the door of which was a tarnished brass plate bearing the inscription 'Music Teacher.' Was it imagination or did I hear the sound of scales played on a piano? I peeped through the window. A small girl was bent in earnest endeavour over the keys of an ancient instrument. I wondered if Miss Kemp was still alive, or did some other kindly martinet rule in this humble temple of Apollo?

I moved on and approached the churchyard. The church was unchanged and the grave-stones in their mossy beds leaned this way and that in aged unconcern—veterans that had long lost interest in the vicissitudes of time. I had once thought them frightening and sinister—now they were but old.

Down the inclined street that led to my old school I came to the market square and Cornhill House. The shop wore its gayest attire. Every window was surrounded and festooned by a climbing profusion of children's sun-bonnets, plush mantel borderings, striped flannelettes, brightly hued towellings, and multicoloured cretonnes. Beneath this arched canopy of decorative drapery I passed into the interior of the shop and presently into the living-rooms beyond where I was made very welcome by my father's partner and his wife. Over lunch we talked shop, but all the while I seemed to exist in two dimensions of time. The voice of my host spoke of immediate things, but the pictures on the wall (the lifeboat was still dimly battling with the waves), the ornamental pendants of glass on the mantelshelf, the very chair on which I sat, every familiar aspect of the room spoke to me of a life that I had once known.

After lunch my host took me into the shop where he was anxious to show me a new line he had recently bought, and bubbling over with enthusiasm he exhibited a rail of coats which he said were selling 'like hot cakes.' He pointed out improvements that had been made in the show-room—more light, a new counter, modern show-cases.

Later, when he was closeted in the office to send off the day's orders, I asked, and received, permission to look over the house. I climbed the stairs and, barely glancing at the negro statuettes, visited the room which had been my nursery. The door with its low brass ring handle was just as I had always remembered it, but the room was now a bedroom. I looked out of the window at the lead roof of the bow-window below and recalled how, as a boy, I had once climbed out on it and, greatly daring, jumped to the top of a neighbouring wall. Greatly daring! I smiled at the distortion of memory, for the wall was little more than a foot away.

Leaving the nursery I crossed the corridor to the other part of the house. The narrow stairs that led to what were once the quarters of the assistants (they now lived out) had been widened. I opened the door of the lumber-room expecting to find the headless ladies, the broken toys, the discarded props and stands of the shop, and received my greatest surprise. The room was a bathroom, tiled, spotless, cleansed. Window enlarged, linoleum on the floor, white enamel bath, towels on towel-rail, odour of bath salts. Bluebeard's chamber had become a place of lavation.

I left the house to explore the garden. I walked up the gravel path to the lawn, which was partly enclosed by the walls of the shirt factory. Along one side grew a row of bushy cone-shaped trees which had been planted during my childhood. Now they stood stout and high—green-whiskered, gorbellied giants. On the other side of the lawn the tap which leaked still dripped from the end of the thin iron pipe and the grass beneath was as usual wet and slippery. The old pear-tree had grown rather more gnarled and twisted and seemed to be in a different position. Then I noticed that the walls of the factory had been extended and this had altered the perspective of both tree and garden.

After a late meal I said good-bye to my kindly hosts and, declining their offer to order the station bus, set off on my return journey to the station on foot. The evening was drawing in, a summer mist rose from the fields, the sun—a glowing, orange ball—rested upon the dark tower of the church.   When I reached the higher ground near the station I turned and looked back, hearing nothing but the silent communication of my thoughts.   W. S. Landor speaking of love says: 'There is a silence in it which suspends the foot.' My foot was now so suspended, for as I looked at the roofs of the town slowly fading from sight in the deepening twilight I knew that I was bidding farewell to something more than the town itself, to something which as the years went by it would be increasingly difficult to recapture.

In the sitting-room the glass which covered the picture of Cornhill House began to dazzle my eyes with the reflected light from the morning sun.   I awoke from my day-dream to hear the steady beat of the pendulum clock above the roll-top desk.   I picked up the deed of partnership, quickly re-read it, and then descended the stairs to join my father in the shop.